THE BIRTH OF EXPERIENCE

THE BIRTH OF EXPERIENCE

Michael Eigen

Routledge
Taylor & Francis Group

LONDON AND NEW YORK

First published 2014 by Karnac Books Ltd.

Published 2018 by Routledge
2 Park Square, Milton Park, Abingdon, Oxon OX14 4RN
711 Third Avenue, New York, NY 10017, USA

Routledge is an imprint of the Taylor & Francis Group, an informa business

Copyright © 2014 to Michael Eigen

The right of Michael Eigen to be identified as the author of this work has been asserted in accordance with §§ 77 and 78 of the Copyright Design and Patents Act 1988.

British Library Cataloguing in Publication Data

A C.I.P. for this book is available from the British Library

ISBN 9781782201533 (pbk)

Edited, designed and produced by The Studio Publishing Services Ltd
www.publishingservicesuk.co.uk
e-mail: studio@publishingservicesuk.co.uk

CONTENTS

ABOUT THE AUTHOR

Michael Eigen worked with disturbed, especially psychotic, children in his twenties, then adults from his thirties onwards. He directed an institute program for working with creative individuals at the Center for Psychoanalytic Training and was the first Director of the Educational Training at the Institute for Expressive Analysis. He was on the board of directors of the National Psychological Association for Psychoanalysis for eight years, first as Program Chair, then as editor of *The Psychoanalytic Review*. He has taught at many institutes and colleges and given talks and seminars internationally. In the past twenty years, he taught and supervised mainly at the National Psychological Association for Psychoanalysis and the New York University Postdoctoral Program in Psychotherapy and Psychoanalysis. He gives a private seminar on Winnicott, Bion, Lacan, and his own work, ongoing for nearly forty years.

The birth of experience goes on all life long. Giving birth to oneself never stops. William James writes of the twice born. The scriptures speak of being born again of the spirit and circumcision of the heart. These are radical changes of state, radical changes of life. But birth of experience also goes on in smaller ways throughout a day or week or year, often barely noticed. Sometimes, it might seem as if experience is in search of an experiencer, one to experience it, dwell with it, grow with it, for it is possible to have new experiences which do not result in growth. One almost goes on as if they did not happen or did not matter much. What does it take to link up with experience that is coming into being? To link up and be further born, undergoing development with experience that is developing and needing attention.

How to get the most out of experience and partner it as it develops is an important challenge, not just individually, but in the social body as well. We are challenged to grow capacity to facilitate growth of experience. Richness of living, in part, depends on it.

The feel and taste of experience is not quite the same in childhood or youth or middle or old age. Variations and mixes are endless. Now, as an older person, experience keeps opening faster and more fully than any time in my life. I have asked myself why this is so and one factor is the reality of experiencing a more distilled sense of experience itself.

So much life is mixed with have to's: have to do this, have to do that, tasks and worries. One gets lost not only with tasks, but also with people and the swim of events. Of course, life tastes differently depending on who one is with and how. Meeting people brings new life into life. Yet, over time, I can say that a sense of experience itself has come more to the fore, sensitivity to the taste of life, the feel of things, the taste of oneself.

Freud called consciousness a sense organ for the perception of psychical qualities. I think of some kind of organ that permeates body and psyche, physical and psychical cells and pores, a capacity to perceive and feel feeling. Kabbalah speaks of many souls and capacities, Kundalini of multiple *chakras*, centres of experience. When we tune into changing centres, what is it we tune in with? Our tuner-in capacity is very special. For me, old age has quickened it.

Perhaps it has to do with not wanting the same things I once did earlier in life: a shift of focus. I think of Yeats' phrase, "soul clap its hands and sing". For Kabbalah, somewhat like Aristotle, there are souls at more physical, emotional, intellectual, intuitive, and mystical levels. William Blake called the body a soul, perhaps a further meaning of "body-ego". Proprioception and kinaesthesia, the very feel of muscle sensation make us feel alive (Wiener, 2011). Sensation adds colour to life, is part of life's colours. We feel more alive or dead, or combinations of aliveness–deadness at any given time. The Bible says the soul is in the blood, in part the kind of soul-blood that fascinated D. H. Lawrence. The Kabbalah Tree of Life (see Chapter One, Figure 1) suggests endless fields of experience are part of any of its capacities. The Zen master raises one finger—all of reality and infinity in a very special finger. Dogen said one sees the reflection of the moon in all the dewdrops. What is this wondrous sense of experience?

It is said that God creates many angels that come and go in an instant. They are present for a moment, then are gone. I wonder if this expresses something about certain moments that come and go— moments of beauty, terror, need, curiosity, wonder. A moment that bursts for an instant, giving all it has, then gone. We are left to wonder if we really felt and saw a shooting star flash through our beings or did we imagine it?

Job ultimately says of God, "I know you in my flesh". What kind of knowing is this? In old age, as in my youth, I love planet earth, colours, sky, water, those close to me and many far away, trinkets, grass, and autumn leaves, sun, moon, music, art, depth psychology—you name it. But a love of the invisible has grown. A love I cannot pin down. I used to locate it in my chest. But now it is more elusive. It can be anywhere. A sense of the invisible keeps growing.

Chuang Tzu writes of all the bells and whistles of life, everything we need to do and all that captures our attention, pushes, crushes, uplifts, then says,

> I do not know what makes them the way they are. It would seem as though they have some True Master, and yet I find no trace of him. He can act—that is certain. Yet I cannot see his form. He has identity but no form. (1964, p. 33)

Love of the invisible, part of the birth of experience that has no end. Love of surface, love of depths, love of the visible, love of the invisible. Wherever you are, there is more.

Chapter One, "Beauty and destruction" is the fifth and last of the series of seminars on Kabbalah and Psychoanalysis I gave for the New York University Postdoctoral Contemplative Studies Project from 2010 to 2013. The first two are expanded in *Kabbalah and Psychoanalysis* (2012a), the third and fourth in *A Felt Sense: More Explorations of Psychoanalysis*, and *Kabbalah* (2014). "Beauty and destruction" opens with a meditation on Beauty, *Tiferet*, the heart of the Tree of Life (Chapter One, Figure 1). Beauty runs through life along with disaster. We say spontaneously, "What a beautiful day!" The beauty of the world and culture touches our mind and heart in so many ways. When Wittgenstein was dying, he said to his care-taker, "Tell them I had a beautiful life." To say and mean this near the moment of death after the torment he went through—what is this beauty that so often makes a difference even in hell?

My chapter, "Tears of beauty and pain: mixed voices", in *Contact With the Depths* (2011a) charts the therapy of a psychotic man as his creative capacities are engaged and grow, involving the dual reality of beauty and pain, at times the pain of beauty. Our meditation on beauty takes us through the shadow of death to a place that feels, if not redemptive and saving, alive and good enough—*Dayenu* ("enough"). William Blake defines enough as too much. He has in mind an uplifting moment or dimension of the soul–body touched by one's divine imagination. Marion Milner quoted the poet Thomas Traherne, feeling that even perception was a form of imagination, and for Blake perception was infinite (Eigen, 2011a). We live an imaginative body that cannot help creating more life as long as it can.

We touch Beauty as the heart of the Kabbalah tree of experiential capacities, its streams spreading in all directions. Towards the end of his life, Bion also speaks of the beauty of psychoanalysis. In one of our sessions, he surprisingly said, "I use the Kabbalah as a framework for psychoanalysis." Once one begins to look at the interplay of Bion and Kabbalah, interweaving themes become obvious. Meldings of faith and catastrophe, problems with sustaining capacity to experience emotional intensity (in Kabbalah, experiential capacities break under intensity of flow), Bion's notations F in O, T in O, his linking of faith and transformation going on in unknown reality (O), movements between fragmentation and creation, the role of fragmentation in creation, to name some main ones (Eigen, 1998, 2012a, 2014).

One might think that going through psychoanalytic difficulties can be grim, and maybe they can be. Yet, at the end of Bion's seminars in New York, after all we went through together, he said, "How is it we experience such joy going through the hard places we have?" The seminar was less than two years before his death. He also added, "At least you will know what it is like having a patient like me." There are many ways to exercise oneself. Psychic exercise has its own special hair-raising aspects and deep satisfactions.

Psychoanalysis can be beautiful. Two people together facing the worst, more often than not, coming through, over and over again, in some way that makes a difference. Even small differences can be big differences in this work. Often, we do not know exactly what is happening or how, but sense something—again this sensing quality, an emotional sensor, a sense of the living psyche.

Both Winnicott and Bion write of dreams having to do with the realness of life, a paradoxical statement, considering that dreams and reality are often opposed. At the same time, we may say of a dream, it felt real, more real than much daily experience. Bion and Winnicott add to this cultural experience, for example, art, literature, religion, as if processes that inform dreaming inform aspects of creative life. Bion gives as an example Falstaff, whom he feels more real to him than many people he meets. A fictional character created by the human mind, alive for the psyche, pulsing with dream elements.

To dream life into being, dream self and experience into being. Winnicott's central clinical preoccupation is feeling unreal to oneself. He searches for and delineates conditions that mediate real-isation, personalisation of experience, particularly birth of one's own sense of realness. One of Bion's central preoccupations involves lack of capacity to tolerate intensity of experiencing, inability to endure the latter's build-up. He depicts shattering and emptying and a variety of ways we die out in face of emotional impacts, or kill ourselves off in order to live (Eigen, 1998, 2011a). Therapy, in part, involves supporting build-up and birth of experiencing.

For Bion, dreaming helps call attention to emotional experience in need of digestion and plays an early role in these digestive processes (Eigen, 2001b). Damaged dreamwork plays a role in chronic emotional indigestion. Along with dream, myth, art, music, literature, and other areas of creative living can be part of a psychic digestive system working through the ages.

Chapter Two, "On the birth of experience", goes into these and many other processes involving birth and growth of experience. Near the beginning of *The Zohar* there is a saying, "There is a rose. And there is a rose!" I interpret this as referring to different qualities of aliveness, so there are ways in which a rose by any other name is not just a "rose". There is more emphasis in Chapter One on Kabbalah and in Chapter Two on psychoanalysis, although in both chapters the two domains meet and intertwine almost seamlessly. In so far as we succeed in letting psyche speak, domains open that are not confine-able by the tools at hand, one reason, as a species, we call ourselves toolmakers, as experience and the tools we use for it become part of further birth processes.

Beauty and destruction

[A meditation bell sounds to call attention to the beginning of the meeting.]

" I t's my pleasure to welcome you. I'm James Ogilvie and on behalf of the Contemplative Studies Project of the New York University Postdoctoral Program I want to welcome you for the ongoing bell that rings and rings and rings from Mike Eigen. Some of you saw the announcement that Mike was promising an adventure today. Mine started on the way down, finding my way through the bike tour the city scheduled, and thinking about the caesura of Sixth Avenue that could not be crossed. So it has got me in a very receptive mood and I'm sure we're in for a real treat today. So without taking anymore time I just want to welcome you and thank Mike again for being here with us today." [Applause]

* * *

I don't know how many of you have played with meditation bells, but, you know, after it seems to stop, it is still going on. Before our Passover *Seder*, I sound a Korean gong and have the children put their ears close to it after it can no longer be heard. You should see their faces when they hear the quiet waves of sound continuing and continuing, fading that never seems to stop. More, more. The quieter it gets, it is still going. And then, special silence.

As is the tradition of the NYU Postdoctoral Contemplative Studies Project, we'll do a short meditation. I wish I could talk like the bell. Well, I'll give short verbal cues for your own bells.

Last time (Eigen, 2014) we did a guided meditation with *Chochma*, wisdom. Today we will do *Tiferet* (see Figure 1) beauty, the heart *sephira*, heart *chakra*.

[Speaking slowly with many pauses.]

Tiferet, Beauty, Heart
Good heart, bad heart
Now only good heart

Beauty gives rise to faith
Supports faith, is part of faith
You may hurt inside
Sorry for bad you have done
Or was done to you
Beauty is beyond that
A beautiful day, a beautiful sky
A moment of wonder

Your pain tells you you're alive
Now, for a moment,
Let Beauty touch your pain,
Let Beauty spread through your pain,
All your pain.
There are so many crevices in pain
And Beauty can find them.
Beauty all through you
Your most secret places

For this moment
Let Beauty give you everything you need.
Let Beauty teach you.
Let the heart of Beauty be your teacher.

We'll sit quietly for a few minutes, feeling Beauty's glow, spreading all through you.

* * *

In Kabbalah, in psychoanalysis, there are many visions. Each talks about states of being, states of mind, capacities, tendencies. Last time, we talked about five souls in Kabbalah, five souls and four worlds (Eigen, 2012a, 2014). But in each of those worlds and in each of those souls, there are infinities of more souls and worlds. And if you look at the sephirot (Figure 1), the skeletal picture leaves everything out. In each *sephira* are all the other *sephirot*. In each *sephira* exists an infinity, an endless infinity, of all the other *sephirot*. A formula might be: in each are all.

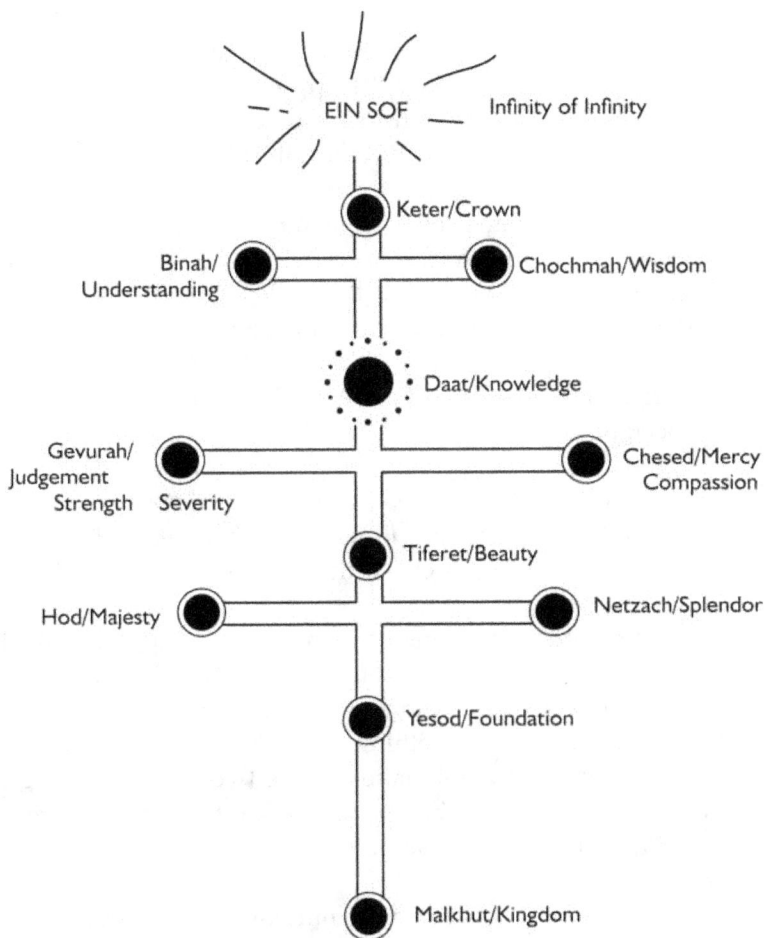

Figure 1.   Ein Sof and the *Sephirot* (Tree of Life).

Kabbalah envisions these as divine capacities, the way God oper-ated in order to create us and the world. Did God actually use these functions, these capacities to create everything? One might imagine God can create any thing any way, with nothing, no means at all, just by virtue of Godness alone. That we share Godly creative capacities is an amazing vision, but we are also aware that when we attribute things to God we are usually, in some way, talking about ourselves.

The crown of the *sephirot* Tree of Life (Figure 1) is *Keter*. Let's sup-pose *Keter* is intuition. In my last talk, I spoke of inner *Keter* as faith, and outer *Keter* as will, divine will, hidden will, mysterious will. Turn the *Keter*-scope, and you have intuition as well. My personal favourite is to begin the top of the tree with Faith. The Tree of Life is the Tree of Faith. But let's not underestimate the importance of intuition, which plays an important role in psychoanalysis, emphatically with W. R. Bion, who has resonant links with Kabbalah (Eigen, 2012a, 2014).

The second *sephira* is *Chochma*, wisdom, followed by Bina, under-standing. *Da'at*, knowledge, comes next, although it is not usually an official *sephira*. Wisdom, understanding, knowledge—the so-called intellectual functions, at the top of the philosophical tree of ancient Greece. Boundaries between them and intuition are fluid. There are passages in which Bion speaks of looking for a spark or seed of wisdom in the rubble, the weeds, the ramble of the psyche. So, the head and neck of the tree: intuition–intellect.

Next come emotional levels and qualities. *Chesed*, mercy, love, associated with the right hand, *Gevurah*, strength, judgement, severity, fear with the left. Between *Chesed* and *Gevurah* is *Tiferet*, Beauty, the sixth *sephira*, associated with chest, the heart of the tree, a balance between the two preceding capacities.

The right side of the tree is felt to be masculine–expansive, the left feminine–restrictive, but there is a lot of room for reversals and mixes. The centre line represents a balancing, harmonising function. But it is more than that. I see it as something creative, as when two qualities create a third. Not just a combination of the two, but something not quite the same as either, something new, a kind of birthing process. Mixtures of qualities and capacities creating further qualities and capacities.

The next set, *sephirot* seven through nine, are *Netzach*, right hip and leg, which I will call persistence or endurance; *Hod*, left hip and leg, which I am calling plasticity, flexibility, openness to spirit. In

Kabbalah, both *Netzach* and *Hod* are involved with prophecy. The rabbis tended to see prophecy as inferior to *Chochmah*, wisdom and the intellectual function, the latter more constant. Prophecy comes and goes, but study and use of intellect is more reliable.

Yesod, foundation, is linked with fecundity. Spiritual, emotional, intellectual, and physical fertility. Traditionally associated with the phallus, which Lacan might appreciate. I call it the Freudian triangle. On one level, *Netzach* is associated with drive, *Hod* with adjusting means toward ends (skilful means), *Yesod* a foundational creativity that runs through the tree.

The tenth *sephira*, *Malchut*, associated with feet, represents the space–time, material reality we live in. The ground we stand on with our own two feet. Wiener (2011), among others, emphasises the psychological importance of our feet in contact with the ground. There are phrases in English that emphasise this grounding: "stand on your own feet", "don't have a leg to stand on", or "someone cuts your legs out from under you". In the latter two phrases, emphasis is on trauma, failure to be able to support yourself. This can be extended to not being able to support your psychic life as well. Lack of support is an important theme in the life of feeling.

From one point of view, you can understand the *sephirot* tree as a descent from immaterial to more material, from the more ineffable to space–time functions, which I often happen to find ineffable too (Eigen, 2006). Jung's four functions roughly parallel its structure: intuition, intellect, feeling, sensation. Husserl's three egos broadly fit, too: transcendental ego, psychological ego, empirical ego. The empirical ego is our space–time, everyday world, everyday reality, "just plain me". The psychological ego is me being aware of my states, a second level of consciousness. What a relief to be just plain me, time off from psychological hyper-awareness. In a way, Husserl has a Kabbalistic element. The transcendental ego constitutes the psychological ego that constitutes the empirical ego: a system of descent. From another vertex, one can put a double arrow between descent ↔ ascent as mutually constitutive.

Above *Keter* are infinite supernal realms, ineffable realms. Infinite infinities. And included in them are infinite dimensions of nothing, emptiness, hiddenness. At the beginning of our day, James talked about the impassable caesura of Sixth Avenue. Well, in Kabbalah, no caesura is totally impassable, although some caesuras are so endless that you can never get to the bottom of them. They remain a mystery, secret. You cannot go as far as caesuras and the worlds go. Something always remains hidden. Remains hidden at the unknown, mysterious top, and remains hidden all through the tree to us. It can feel that the distance between oneself and the Divine is impassable, yet points of contact remain. Distances within ourselves might also seem impassable, with intimations of inaccessible links. We remain hidden, not transparent to ourselves, not fully. We cannot be conscious of all the processes that make us up. The psalms are moving expressions of our lack of transparency: out of the depths I call, / You know my hidden places better than I know myself.

According to the *sephirot* scheme, our knowing K-self and cognitive capacities descend from *Ein Sof*, that which is without bounds, limitless. Our sense of knowledge is touched by infinity. No-thing gives rise to things, *Ayin* (nothing) gives rise to *Yesh* (being). A system of emergent functions, capacities, states, souls, worlds.

If I graphed the five souls, you would have: (1) a vital soul, *nefesh*, associated with our space–time world (*Malchut*); (2) an emotional soul, *ruach* (*Sephirot* 4–9; *Chesed* through *Yesod*, higher and lower emotions); (3) an intellecual soul, *neshama* (*Chochma, Binah, Da'at*), (4) an intuitive soul, *chaya* (*Keter* and aspects of supernal worlds); and (5) a special soul essence, *yechida*, a point in contact with an essence point of *Ein Sof*. These delineations are not hard and fast. For example, *Binah* (understanding) is often associated with intuition. And certain forms of intuition run through the tree's trunk and branches.

A note on *yechida*, soul essence conjoined with God's essence. A persistent immediacy, as when it says in the *Seder*, "God took you out of Egypt, not an angel, not a messenger, God Himself". A soul-point free of limitations. We are paradoxical beings. Limited and in despair over limitations. With work and luck, we learn how to use our capacities. We learn how to use ourselves creatively, creative limits. But there are also moments of no-limit, moments of Grace past the struggle. Three dimensions: just plain me, struggle, and Grace. All dimensions at once, now more one than another, fluctuations, oscillations with variable combinations and emphases.

A little background note. There is disagreement as to when Kabbalah originated. Some say with Abraham, some say with Adam. There were threads of Jewish mysticism BCE and many important visions and discussions early in CE. But the efflorescence of what is ordinarily called Kabbalah seems to have been in twelfth and thirteenth century Southern France and Spain, with important waves in sixteenth century Israel–Palestine.

The Chassidic movement that grew in eighteenth century Russia emphasised emotional aspects of worship and psychological aspects of spiritual growth. Psychological types and groups might place more emphasis on intellect and/or emotion. Chassidus was steeped in Kabbalah and reworked it creatively, with important interpretations and additions throughout the twentieth century. When I say Kabbalah, I am often including important contributions of Chassidus and when I say Chassidus, I am probably including Kabbalah. I make this note to forestall criticism that I am confusing Kabbalah and Chassidus. I am aware of the intermingling and co-fertilisation and often use both my way. Jewish mysticism blends *Torah*, *mishnah*, *talmud*, Kabbalah, and Chassidus and more.

For me, Moses meeting God on Mount Sinai is a centre of the *Torah*. To meet God. Who would have thought so many laws would come out of this meeting, a meeting that takes us beyond limitations, a mystical moment *par excellence*. Before the afterglow fades, all the have to's begin. You have to do this x times, you have to do that y times. Yet, limitations were built into the meeting itself. Moses says, I want to see You, I want to see Your face. Perhaps God tries to protect Moses by saying you can see my backside as I flash by. Perhaps God knew what Moses did not, that we do not have the equipment to see God straight on without burning up in a flash. You can experience God's glory but I am not sure you can see it. One of Job's remarks, "I know you in my flesh". Face to face with God might be more than we can endure. Perhaps a little like Krishna in the *Gita*, unbearably monstrous in his unadorned, revealed presence. Even full radiance of Beauty might be too much. Yet, God praises Moses in the *Torah* and says that they talked face to face. But, on Mount Sinai, God shields man's face from the full intensity of the meeting. Moses experienced much, but, again, with limitations. Not seeing God face to face was akin to not entering the Promised Land.

Some time ago, I saw an advertisement for a night at the Ruben Museum, a New York City museum of Tibetan Buddhist art. The invitation was to sleep overnight under one of the paintings and in the morning discuss your dreams with a psychoanalyst. That might be one way to build tolerance for more experiencing of a profoundly uplifting, challenging kind.

Perhaps Moses experiences as much as he can take, and then some. God says, hide in this crevice of the rock and you can glimpse my backside going by. You can see God's back, not face. I often thought of this as God flashing his tushy. Burning to a crisp when trying to get closer to God is something that happened to Aaron's sons. But I wonder, is burning and becoming one with the Flame such a bad way to go? It might also symbolise a heightened moment of self-nullification when all there is is God.

There is a lot of commentary on this. For some, seeing God's back means Moses can see the *dalet* (Hebrew letter "d") that knots the back of the head *tefilin*. *Tefilin*—phylacteries worn on head and arm with scriptures in them. Even God wears *tefilin* (perhaps to remind him He is God or of his God-function, or simply as part of the devotional substratum of being). *Tefilin* straps are laced or knotted to form the letters *shin* ("s"), *dalet* ("d"), and *yud* ("y"), standing for Shaday, a God-name often meaning God Almighty.

Another view is that the knot on the back of the head *tefilin* God wears has to do with wrestling. A knot of struggle, perhaps within God, with God, or within ourselves. Earlier, I noted three experiences of life: just plain everyday me, struggle, and Grace. At the level of struggling with oneself, one might feel, I don't like the way I am, I want to be a better person, a less hurtful person. Is there anything I can do about it? In some respects, it does not look as if there is. I will never get rid of all that is wrong, not within me, not outside me. I cannot "cure" myself or the world, but perhaps I can do *something* about it. Perhaps I can work with it, have some modulating effect. Because I cannot cure it does not mean I can do nothing. One has to try. I am not always my worst self. I manage to protect some people some of the time from my most monster-Krishna-Yahweh self.

So, we struggle. Some rabbis say Moses represents struggle. They do not use the word struggle, but tend to use the word affliction. We are told on Yom Kippur, Day of Atonement, to afflict ourselves, penitential self-affliction. Life afflicts us—affliction is one of life's modes of experience and affliction itself has many nuances and functions. One scenario is that affliction, or the part of you afflicted, stops you from seeing clearly. It could be a minor or major affliction. There is a story about the Israelites in a time of trouble asking a prophet, should they go to Egypt or not. In the bible, Israel sought refuge in Egypt more than once. This time, the prophet answered no.

Well, when a prophet says something, he has to verify it, he has to listen to himself: is that me speaking or God? It is hard being a prophet. Jesus said, you will know them by their fruits. But a prophet himself? How does he know? In a few years, this particular prophet came to realise that he spoke out of selfish need, not on behalf of God. His wishes affected his judgement: "I didn't want to leave because I wanted my son to follow my calling, and one can only be a prophet in the Holy Land." Another seer he consulted reinforced his realisation, telling him his son would not have the distinction of being a prophet, a fact hard to digest, but the ring of truth. The prophet reversed his decision, advising the people to go and take refuge, coming to grips with the truth that his ambitions for his son were not to be fulfilled.

In so many ways, we meet this tension between particular needs or desires and larger facts of life. We are called to struggle with ourselves in countless ways. Moses and Yahveh represent the dimension of struggle, made up of many dimensions. For one, the struggle between good and evil, our better and worse aspects, conflicts our dual nature gets us into. Mystical Judaism speaks of good and evil inclinations, associating the latter with our animal soul and the former with spiritual soul. I suspect it is not so easy (not that this binary is easy). Traditionally, Satan also is spirit. Evil thoughts are not only part of animal mind (in mythic and pictorial portrayals, Satan and his correlates span animal and spirit mind). Affective attitudes that influence our lives come as much from the top down as from the bottom up (Eigen, 1986).

*   *   *

As a footnote, something I never cared for, the idea of the Hebrews being God's favourite people, the chosen ones. For me, some rabbinic additions can be chilling, particularly the idea that Israel has heart and the *goyim*, the "nations", at best pretend to have heart but are essentially heartless and selfish. God has always played favourites. Cane and Abel, Esau and Jacob, the list twists and turns through history. Commentary rationalises this by seeing dual strains in our nature, more fully God-hearted *vs.* selfish, a double thread. Even in heaven, some saints are closer to God than others because of their merits or God's likings.

From the earliest time, I felt we are all God's children. The idea of favourites felt foreign to me, but I understood it as expressive of our nature. What is your favourite this, your favourite that? A parent's favourite child. Once I asked Francesca Bion which of her husband's books was his favourite, Mine, at the time, was *Attention and Interpretation*, which I read and taught for many years. I thought it the climax of his work. She surprised me by saying she did not think he had a favourite, they were all his favourites, his babies. Winnicott's writing on transitional experience tells us we do have favourites, our *own* transitional objects. My *own* world. My *own* people. My truth, as if one can own truth. The double meaning of own is striking, referring to self-feeling, existence of self, and ownership, as if we own ourselves when owning self is far from what we do. Once again, the Bible mirrors tendencies that remain problematic all life long.

Everyone has a comparison mind. It is part of being able to make distinctions necessary for living. But "own self" blows it out of proportion. Today we are bombarded with pictures of super-plenty and super-lack. It is hard to find an orientation that fits one's life. Not too big, not too small—a right enough frame of reference. The Bible speaks of being happy with one's portion. When I first heard that as a child, something rested inside me. I felt relief, because deep down it was something I felt but did not know. It was never recognised, had nowhere to go. You were not supposed to be satisfied when there could be more. Well, more is an important part of life. But there can also be a deep area of content with the gift of self and life one has.

So, Moses, too, had his problems. He is called the greatest prophet of Israel but did not merit entering the Promised Land. He could not get as close to God as he wanted. And, as I have often written (2001a, 2002), there were problems in Eden. There is much in religion that is parochial, gendered, racist. I have my own way of living with things. Sometimes, things I cannot live with, I change their meaning. We are all favourite people—if favourite has to come into it. We are all God's chosen children in our portions, as the case may be. In so far as one uses a God-frame, problems of portions, shorter or longer lives, better or worse existences and conditions will never be solved. There is no understanding of inequalities in such a frame. Nevertheless, I find so much meaning in spiritual texts that open doors of my experience that I gain all I can from them, even if I have to adjust them to who and where I am now. They are filled with observations of human existence, states, tendencies, capacities, emotions. If one looks aright and turns the key, wisdom dimensions appear.

We have infinite holy modes and infinite unholy modes. Ego and self modes, no-self, no-ego modes. More one or the other at a given time, gradations, continua, permutations. When I see the permutations fractals make, I think of the even more amazing permutations of states and capacities our nature produces. It is not a contradiction to feel at one with one's "portion" and thrilled by possibilties, known and unknown. Each and every portion has infinite experiential possibilities—including the implicit possibilities in dying.

Moments of being closer to God, then closer still. Moments in the holy land within, the holy land soul, and beyond. I have spoken of three broad experiential levels (there are more): just plain me, constant struggle, Grace. Moses is the level of constant struggle, the binaries, good and bad. The dimension of Grace is beyond binaries, no place at all. St Paul asks in such moments, where is body, mind, spirit? There's only Grace. For that moment, no death, no evil, just Grace. You could be a bastard or a saint. It does not matter. You do not have to earn it. It just is. If God wants you to have this moment, to be this moment, it happens. God can do this with anyone, anytime. You might call this a oneness dimension, but that does not express it. It is beyond "oneness". It is a state, a blessing we have, can have. Even if you are filled with pus and venom, you are not foreclosed from moments of grace. A Zen Buddhist saying: "There are good days even in hell".

The *Seder* image of being taken out of Egypt, *mitzrayin*, the world of limitations expresses a grace moment. A moment beyond which is also the most inside moment of all. It all drops away, your crippled self, your shells, everything you wanted not to be. Heaven can happen anytime. One might say, a taste of heaven. But that taste carries a bit of the whole and with that bit you feel *dayenu*, more than enough. Not that there is not or cannot be more. But each bit is infinite, each portion has its own infinities.

It can happen anytime, occasioned by anything. Buddha sitting with suffering, with total intensity, then a moment's opening. Was it occasioned by seeing the stars at night or by a woman giving him a cup of milk? Nirvana—Grace. Another plane of existence. The shell of existence lifted.

Although Moses represents dimensions of rules and laws and struggle, he has mystical moments, the climactic Mount Sinai, meeting God face to face, almost. Everything follows from this moment. Another rabbinic meaning given to seeing God's backside is that back means past. An important part of Moses' prophetic vision was seeing the past, seeing what God made of the past, all the actions of the past. Yet, there were ways he could not see the present, ways the present is unknown. The unknown present becomes a psychoanalytic method for Bion, who describes the psychoanalytic attitude as being without memory, expectation, desire, or understanding, F in O, an attitude of responsive faith, open to impacts of unknown present reality. The fact that the present is unknown evokes an experience of limitless depth.

We are speaking about states, gradations and qualities of states, experiential moments, dimensions of experience. We love to study the past. We might not have prophetic vision like Moses, but we are keenly interested in our story. We are thrilled to get hints, even though we differ in interpretations. I recently heard that archaeologists had exhumed a temple that existed some four thousand years ago in Iraq, possibly about the time of Abraham. Wonderful to speculate about existence then, the scent of the human, excited by artefacts, signs of life. We are fascinated with the way our brain works in a similar way. We learn a lot about the workings of the physical universe, our bodies, our brains, yet it is still a mystery. Our knowledge is a bit like learning how to turn a light on and off with a switch but knowing little about what electricity is.

Rabbis imagine Moses sees a knot in the *tefilin* in the back of God's head, the knot of the past exciting the present. Homo spiritus, the knotted being. Apparently, Moses had his own knots, at times represented by an anger problem. It is no accident that Michelangelo's Moses and Freud's writings on it depicted intense conflict with emotion, searing tension.

The level of Grace seems to be tension free, although sustaining any experience requires a certain degree of tension. Bion brings out how difficult it is for us to sustain the build-up of emotional intensity, as if we are partly embryonic in the capacity to support experience. Perhaps one of the characteristics of a grace moment is its capacity to support *us*.

If Moses is associated with judgement, some rabbis associate Rabbi Akiva with mercy. There seems to be some hint that mercy is part of Grace, but, as noted earlier, I would hesitate to reduce Grace to binaries. It is said that had Akiva been in the priestly courts, no one would have ever been sentenced to death. Akiva, for many years, was my favourite rabbi. I talked about him in our first seminar three years ago (Eigen, 2012a). He is one of those identified by the rabbis as being closer to mercy than judgement. Binaries are difficult. Think of all the time Moses pleaded with God to be merciful rather than severe with his people. Yet, he is the law-giver and Akiva is the perfect lamb, at once transcendent, hallowing, inspired. It is important to internalise that you should not kill, but Akiva is known as giving all as he was killed, a different form of self-giving and surrender than Moses underwent. Each touches different nuances of self or soul or personality.

I have heard different versions of what Akiva said as he was being skinned alive and/or burned at the stake, or crucified by the Romans. He died with God on his lips, One, *Echad*. But also with a sense that now he was giving everything, any drop of what had been held back. To love God with all one's heart and soul and might. Everything one possesses, everything that possesses him. Self-giving with nothing left out, a perfect moment beyond all perfect moments.

The saving moment takes lots of forms, between Moses' murdering an Egyptian taskmaster and beginning a journey that would lead to a new kind of "freedom" (being bound to God, a vision or sense of God in every Jewish soul) and Akiva's surrendering transformation of a torturous end. Between assertion and surrender.

Along a somewhat different, but not totally unrelated, vein, a story of "outsider" art, if true. The artist, Edward Deeds, an inmate in a mental hospital, created his art on hospital stationery. At some point, when older and perhaps feeling there was not much time left, he stitched his work together on leather in order to preserve it and gave it to his family for safekeeping. When his family sold their house, they forgot about his work in the attic and the next owners put it out in the rubbish. A young college student walking by noticed the leather, something that caught his eye, and salvaged the work. He showed it to art experts who liked it, valued it. If you look closely at some of his drawings you see notations, a repeated message: ECT, help. You can find more about this arresting story on the *Huffington Post*.

Why mention Edward Deeds' story now? It strikes me as a good example of a creative spirit that does not die, cannot be wiped out even by the most dire circumstances (although perhaps it can). The Moses story is about an enslaved people gaining freedom, a story that never ends. In human beings, tensions between slavery–freedom seesaw. The outcome is never settled once and for all. Challenges, vicissitudes remain. The "freedom" the Hebrew people gained against the backdrop of "slavery" was relative. As Freud said at the end of a tape about psychoanalysis near the end of his life, "The struggle is not yet over". The question in many lives, sometimes, is: to what extent can it begin (Berdyaev, 1944)?

Edward Deeds in a mental hospital, eroded by ECT, managed to find a way to express himself. An area of freedom, small perhaps from the outside, but moments of struggle and grace from the inside. In part, I envision this as a *Shechina* cry from the depths of *Malchut*. It is said about the Hebrews as slaves in Egypt, that they reached the forty-ninth level of depravity. Had they gone down one more step, even God could not save them. But they cried out and the journey began. There is no one-to-one parallel between Deeds and Israel in slavery. But they share a common structure: beauty, creativity emerging from the depths. For Deeds, drawing was an opening in a world of closed doors. He put what he could of himself into it.

We speak of messages in bottles thrown out to sea. I think that is a good image for something in us. Perhaps the message is a most private part of self, incommunicado self, as Winnicott calls it, hidden treasure in hell. Perhaps I am saying that even in slavery, in hell, in electroconvulsive shock, a measure of grace continues. Can that be? For me, it is a most basic fact of life.

* * *

A part of the soul in ineffable Grace. Or should I say there are Grace souls, struggle souls, everyday souls, hell souls, sorrow souls, joy souls. In *Ecstasy* (2001a), I wrote about feeling sandwiches, glad–mad–sad sandwiched together, for example. Akiva's death is an instance of Grace even in hell. For rabbis, he represents a higher level of transcendence than Moses, who links more with reward–punishment (although there is a lot of variation). A suggestion here is that there is something in you beyond reward and punishment, beyond right and wrong, true and false, good and bad, something that just is beautiful. Grace beyond words, ineffable, inexpressible. Grace that lifts you and you feel, "Oh my God, I wish I could feel like this forever." And maybe, in a way, you are feeling that forever now, a thread of your being, a special layer of the sandwich. It is often occluded by all the things you are because you cannot be one thing too long unless you are wretched. People who fall into deep depression seem to testify that you can be wretched longer than you can be happy. But states keep changing, although sometimes the change is very slow.

Bion says that in "pathological" splitting it is much harder to change states than in "normal" splitting. I am not too happy about the words "pathological–normal", but he touches real experience. Staying with our changing states can make us happy, if we are not pummelled too much by big waves. There are lots of ways to evoke and go with changing states that keep a good thread going. Meditate, loosen up, go swimming, stand on our heads, say hello, not hold on to grudges—there are so many possibilities. Often life provides nuanced changes that take us by surprise. Often, I am lifted by strangers, someone on the subway who seems at one with himself, expressive, speaking with his feeling self. Last week, I saw a man standing still as a statue in meditation beneath a tree in Prospect Park, unmoving, steadfast stillness that is breathtaking. Between stillness and expressiveness. Momentary experiences that feel like models for experience.

*   *   *

Cain and Abel. Why did Cain kill his brother? Why did God let him off so lightly considering the gravity of his crime? What is the mark of Cain? Is it a mark many of us feel within us?

Humankind has spoken of something off from near the beginning—perhaps before the beginning. Something good and something bad. On one level, we sum this up by speaking of pleasure and pain and, at another, good and evil. The Garden of Eden was filled with problems. Is the Garden of Eden the other side of the Garden of Evil and vice versa? If murder could happen, it *would* happen. A death sentence for eating of the Tree of Knowledge nurtured fear, curiosity, desire, and death. Death spreads. If God sentenced you to die, you could play God and kill another or yourself. One could speak of the inevitability of consequences flowing from choices, of karma, with or without God. It seems in the Bible that God was often playing God, and people were gods manqué. So much of God's psychology is our psychology.

God marked Cain to protect him, but the mark we feel inside is often other than protection. It is a blemish, a feeling of something wrong, deformed, twisted, warped, at times poisoned. Or worse, mangled, suffocated, pulverised (Eigen, 1998, 2009), both scar and open wound. The mark of Cain burrows deep inside and reminds us we are killers.

I have often heard the phrase, kill or be killed, and the lament, warning, and assessment that this is the kind of world we live in, ignore it at your peril. The mark of Cain runs deep. Perhaps it has achieved partial success as a reminder, a protective warning about ourselves. But it is also a partial failure, for we still kill and are killed. The warning has not stopped us. We are not protected from ourselves.

Yes, Cain was sentenced to be a vagabond. Instead of a tiller of the soil, which was his calling, the land he tilled would be barren. The land within barren—what punishment could be more devastating? The curse of Cain. Akin to the curse of the serpent, to grovel on its belly on the ground. For Cain, a farmer, to be torn from the land, his land. To be torn from his source of nourishment means more than not being able to grow crops. We are also speaking of the nourishment within, what nourishes life, torn, perhaps, from the inner God-source, the root of existence, or from one's own disposition.

Cain is an example of the twice born, something that happens many times in the Bible. One who swerves from his original sensibility, from what comes naturally, to a new life. The image of crossing a river is shared by the Bible and Buddhism. But in Cain's case, his life becomes devoted to building cities. Cain, the builder of cities. Is murder part of building cities, a prerequisite? Not only a capacity for murder, but the act itself? Not once, but many times and often, akin to sexual intercourse (the latter usually a "safe" form of murder called love).

Twists and turns are many. What the Bible calls the beginning of the world four or five thousand years ago might refer to the beginning of Neolithic cities. A tension between animal husbandry and agriculture. We are told we were hunter-gatherers before we were farmers. Was the sacrifice of meat earlier than the sacrifice of crops? Reversal after reversal. Cain, the first born; Abel, the first murdered. As the earlier, ought not Cain to have been a hunter-gatherer and Abel the grower of crops? Time, person, and position often reverse in biblical stories, part of an underlying fluidity of meaning and possibility.

My take: Cain and Abel are a twinship within us, killer and killed. We have both tendencies (Eigen, 2005). The Bible often divides aspects of the self or personality between *dramatis personae*, pairs, brothers, sisters, man and woman. One vision: tendencies experienced as antagonistic and at war might some day also be seen as co-nourishing, mutually supportive. The lion will lie down with the lamb or, better, the two creatively work together. How will we get to this point? To some extent, we are already there. Therapy is one experiment in making the most of competing voices within. Instead of merely pitting one against the other, developing receptivity to the contributions of both. In the birth of cities, division of labour became more imperative. And with complex organisations of systems of co-operation, competition also grew. The latter could be part of the former, an outgrowth of learning to live together in greater numbers. But the Bible teaches us that rivalry is encoded in our makeup, ready for situations to unlock it. A sense of unfairness, injustice, seems part of the background of infancy, subject as every infant is to powerful forces without and within. Some of these forces seem obvious, but we can only guess at others.

Let me share with you another "take" on the Cain–Abel story, a story with wide ramifications for how we work, function, experience. A Jewish mystical view jumps off from the fact that Cain brought his sacrifice first, Abel later. At first glance, this seems a virtue. Cain was avid, quick to want to please God. We are often told to seek and perform *mitzvahs* (commandments, good deeds) with alacrity and joy.

However, this very virtue is seen as a drawback. Abel took more time. This is understood to mean he gave his sacrifice more careful thought, went deeper in trying to fathom what would please God most. He dug deeper in himself. This process of going into the depths was what God savoured. Abel gave more of himself.

Cain might well be miffed. Bringing a sacrifice was his idea. Abel mimicked him. Cain felt he should be rewarded. He spearheaded the movement towards worship. It did not dawn on him that Abel went deeper: nothing could be further from his thought. He was taken in by appearances. Commentaries often take sides when it comes to tensions within binaries, here expressed as affective attitudes towards brothers (Cain bad, Abel good; Esau bad, Jacob good). Sometimes complexities are lost, sometimes thickened (remember, the Bible often works by reversals as well as rigidities).

I know a couple in which the man thinks of the most ingenious presents for the woman, and he often feels hurt because she might not give him any gift for long periods of time. It seems to be his nature to give freely and often, yet she cannot give him as he does her because nothing she thinks of giving satisfies her. She has to find something that she will really be satisfied in giving him. Quick expression *vs.* a slow immersion process. One with flashes, the other cud chewing.

God attempts to awaken Cain to the psychology of Abel, a stewing process foreign to Cain. Perhaps this applies to two sensibilities and also to different tendencies in creative work. Fast flashes on the one hand, slower steeping on the other, both important intrapsychically. Faster and slower processes working together or antagonistically. Going to bat for the first thing that comes or waiting to see what more might develop. Not just first, but second, third, fourth, fifth, sixth thought. With more attention, more opens. Sometimes, speed is important, sometimes waiting. Often, both work together to open experience.

To some extent, the Cain and Abel situation is a kind of failed therapy, to some extent, a transformation journey. Acting fast, sitting with it. Different forms of thinking–feeling–sensing personality tendencies in a person.

In this version of the story, it turns out that God appreciated the care and depth of thought that Abel gave to his gift. A sign to the Cain side of our personality that there is more to do. Cain, the murderer, also cares. He has his own level of devotion, sincerity. An aspect of us wants to be better. What did Cain do wrong (besides literal killing)? He killed the capacity to look into himself more deeply. He substituted reactive anger, jealousy, or envy for more complex experiencing. He did not go into himself far enough, did not think God might have His reasons. God seemed to him as unreflective as he was.

In another story, roles may reverse. But in this particular view, a quicker, more shallow vantage point is pitted against a deeper one. Each has advantages and disadvantages. Fast can be right and slow wrong, too, depending on the moment. In the moment depicted here, God is asking for more self-examination, complexity. Slow down, look at yourself. Walk around your inner self as you would walk around a Rodin sculpture. Give yourself simmering down time. From this vantage point, the story critiques uncritical reactivity.

In the end, therapy occurred, too. Cain had to develop more complexity, reflected in the complexity of cities. But rationalisation of the story as part of a wisdom journey does not take out the primal sting of the fact that we are killers, even if we link killing with growth.

There are many stories of playing favourites in wisdom tales. On one level, they reflect hard facts of life that no amount of sweet talk can undo. Yet, as a psychologist, I find them helpful as markers for different states and tendencies. What seem to be acute inequities also delineate inner tensions, different souls, worlds of experience. Among other things, they portray important affect links. Keep your eye on the affect.

Is the story emphasising a hate link, a drive for ascendency, a need to be on top? Is part of the link humiliation, shame, a sense of defeat and injury? Often subjects shift but the linking affect remains the same: who is killing whom, who is beating whom, who is fighting whom now? Who gets to be boss—now you, now me, this group, that group, this country? What tendency, state, personality organisation dominates you? What are the competing bosses in your personality? The bosses may change, but the boss drive and link keeps working. Who or what is beating whom or what when?

When is it better to be in ascendancy and when is it better to be recessive? We need both tendencies. I have a very stingy feeling when it comes to the psyche: I do not want anything to be lost. All our tendencies may have value in particular contexts. At times, I am a hoarder and hold on to everything. At times, I let everything go. Both tendencies are needed. Our dual tendencies are precious if we can catch on how to work with them.

William Blake writes that all states are eternal and pictures heaven as a state in which all voices of personality have their maximum say and enrich each other rather than injure or destroy.

What's the trick? How do we get to a place where everything contributes? How do we minimise destruction and maximise mutual enrichment?

As suggested earlier, Rabbi Akiva stands for enrichment beyond reward–punishment, beyond struggle, a state Blake might describe as heaven, St Paul as Grace. Think of moments when everything feels all right, when, for a time, no aspect of self is sowing discord. A sense that it all fits together or, better, does not have to fit together, because everything is working not only co-operatively, but creatively, a sense that everything is contributing.

In daily life, sooner or later, you will come across someone who rubs you wrong. Maybe someone in your family, maybe no one you know. Someone you just cannot bear, whether for a shorter or longer time. It could also be likely that you are such a person for someone, near or far.

In our first seminar a couple of years ago (Eigen, 2012a), we noted that Rabbi Nachman depicts a state characterised by war: nations and cities at war, war within families, between and within individuals. A war link or state or tendency. He offers this tendency as an "explanation" as to why some individuals might go crazy when meditating alone in a forest. All alone, there is nothing to save them from warring tendencies within themselves. In such an instance, warring tendencies have nowhere to go and tear the self apart. We need someone to fight with to keep sane. So many stories in the Bible can be used as markers of a warring tendency within. As if observers of human nature, tasters of how it feels to be alive, how it feels to be a person, put a tracer on tendencies that destroy us and tried also to trace some tendencies that further living.

Once tuning into emotional currents in the Bible (or other wisdom literature), a semi-luminous sense of psychic reality emerges. The biblical flood, for example. God personifies a primal reaction to extreme dissatisfaction, like a baby's rage or other emotional flood that drowns everything out, perhaps an attempt to drown out pain. God, disappointed in his creatures, wants to wipe them out and all creation with it. Things are not as good as he wished or imagined. Expectations and vision of life thwarted. Freud called the first trauma flooding, mixtures of outer and inner impingement.

The "total flood" moment is one scenario, but, in actuality, there are variable degrees and qualities of flooding. There are many scenarios and possibilities, for example, wiping out only selective parts of the world, personalities I cannot stand. I am going to try to make this world into one I want to live in. I-as-God will let all the nice people, the ones I like, live—Noah and his family and the animals and plants and . . . But the ones I cannot stand—gone.

In all such scenarios and stories, it does not take long for bad things to start happening again. Look what happened with Noah and his family. In not too long a time bad stuff rose to the surface. We may try in fantasy, or in bits of realistic action, to wipe out evil or bad feeling or injury, but not for long. Where people are, bad and good stuff happens. One could say this of all existence, but it is the human mind or soul or spirit that magnifies and interprets the drama and brings it to other planes. To get rid of all that ails us, we would have to get rid of people.

Therapy is a special instance of being stuck with each other. There are times I might tell someone, "It's just your luck to be stuck with someone like me." Or, "Yes, I can empathise with your wish to see someone else and that might (or might not) be a good idea. But sooner or later, if you're going to be in therapy, it will have to be with someone." The only problem with therapy is that people are involved. There is no escaping human contact and, therefore, no escaping problems and the problematic aspects of life. But, as Rabbi Nachman (Eigen, 2012a) pointed out, if you manage to isolate yourself from contact with others, you are stuck with wars inside yourself. I think of a Sumerian proverb, "I escaped the wild ox only to be confronted by the wild boar". I suspect some people go from one therapist to another to escape the "flood-link", others because they fear discovering how limited we all are.

Stories like the flood dramatise that no matter how you try to start over, sooner or later problems you thought you had escaped loom up in one or another form. Starting over is a biblical theme, characteristic of many stories. We keep trying and there is benefit from the struggle. There are many kinds of starting over along a creative–destructive continuum (Eigen, 1992). In some ways, starting over is aborted, at least partially. Going from one partial abortion to another, one partial birth to another. Utopian wishes keep rising. Hitler's utopian vision, for example, purifying national blood. But bugs keep coming and sooner or later you may have to begin dealing with the fact that you are buggy, too.

Some feel we are trying to eradicate ourselves in order to solve the problem of being human. Most of us prefer a less dramatic solution. The latter may require us to build more of a taste for the unsolvable and appreciate a little movement at a time. Can we become a little less harmful to others and ourselves? Can we do a little more on the just plain me level and use constant struggle as needed? Can the whole enterprise be informed by an overarching or supportive sense of Grace? I see this as an evolutionary challenge.

Question: I'm very troubled by Cain and Abel. On my way here, I was talking to the cab driver about shepherds and farmers still fighting about who gets the best deal. They're always in conflict. But that's not what's troubling me now. I'm still mad at God. Why couldn't God accept both sacrifices? Why did God have to make it so either/or?

Response: You tell me.

Question: Because He should have listened to me and He didn't! He should have listened to His mother! (Laughter.)

Response: Well, you know, there are all kinds of ways to cut the pie. Aren't we speaking about us, our nature? Everything in God is us. We don't get along. We do and don't get along. Sibling rivalry. We hate each other, we love each other. We fight over territory, possessions, love, ego. It depends how the wheel turns at a given time. The problems expressed in biblical stories seem insoluble. There doesn't seem to be much sign of their letting up. We are still waiting on ourselves, working with ourselves. Yet, many factors stop us. As I mentioned, I think we're up against an evolutionary challenge (Eigen, 2008, 2011a).

Question: [Hard to hear on the tape. It concerns Bion's writings on catastrophic reality, psychological realities, surviving catastrophe or not.]

Response: So often in Chasidic texts you find phrases about "the blessed God, the blessed God". The repetition can make me feel there is enormous defence against the cursed God. Blessings and curses. The emotions these words express are part of us, the polarity, the range, the amalgams, the continuum. Different states with variable emphases. I wonder how much of our inner lives are concerned with warding off catastrophe or dealing with actual or anticipated catastrophe. Bion writes that a sense of catastrophe cements personality together. This is especially true of psychotic states, but may be more general. We might have different kinds of psychic cement working together or antagonistically in lots of ways with catastrophic dreads and realities. How omnipresent is catastrophic dread? How do we respond to it? We have a plethora of capacities to work with. We can bite off bits of catastrophic globs and turn raw impacts into images, dream them, reflect on them, create with them. As Bion's work goes on, he tends to emphasise open-ended faith, which might express itself as attention in the present. Attention seems to grow more important for Bion as faith does. To the extent that one can, staying with felt impacts of reality at hand (Eigen, 2014).

Question: I just wanted to add an image, a favourite image of mine. I rethought it when you were talking about the *sephirot* and the feet and the top. Rabbi Abraham Heschel's statement, when he marched with Martin Luther King Jr, arm in arm in the front row of Selma—he said he was praying with his feet. In thinking about this today, I was seeing the infinite of the infinite of each *sephira* turning into a circle with top and bottom joining each other, absorbing all the branches in a single image.

Response: Thank you.

Question: I had a similar image, an astrological association. I'm an astrologist as well as psychoanalyst. Top–bottom connection, intertwining, makes me think of Pisces, associated with the feet. It is also a sign associated with faith, conveying a sense of the boundless unity of all things. With astrology, you start with Aries and go down the body to Pisces. Understanding and feet are associated together. The circle is significant in astrological assignation. Beginning and end, unity and foundation are together.

Response: From the first moment I met Bion, I felt a sense of the word understanding to be standing under. When I looked at him, I felt he was standing under me. I can't convey this unassuming sense of deep support. I had at least five or six feelings at the same time, a bunch, a pack. One of them was that he was standing under me and I felt immediately released to try to get help. Under rather than over me— you feel the difference

Some twenty or so years later, in *Ecstasy* (2001a) I spoke of a feeling sandwich, for example, a mad–glad–sad sandwich. While in Japan, I went to a temple for Kwan Yin (Kannon, Kanzeon), a Buddha of compassion. Kwan Yin cannot be anything but compassionate. In several sculptures, Buddha after Buddha were stacked on top of each other, including Buddha demons. I imagined I saw an avatar of a destructive force Bion described, a force that can only destroy, that goes on detroying after everything is destroyed, it can do nothing else. The counterpart of Kwan Yin, who can be nothing but be compassionate and wants nothing in recompense for granting favours, save thank you. I imagined Bion's destructive force as a Buddha in the stack. And on the very top of the pile was Kwan Yin. I felt this was a kind of Buddha sandwich, Kwan Yin sandwich, in which all the forces and tendencies of personality are working under the aegis of compassion, each with their special contributions channeled through an overarching or subtending attitude expressed in Kwan Yin.

* * *

[Intermission]

During the break, someone spoke about feeling mostly negative about the knot for much of her life. As the morning went on, she began getting more of a realisation that struggle is not just a negative, something you have to slog through, but that it is also a point of contact with God. The struggle has an uplifting dimension as well as a crushing dimension, partly depending on attitude as well as circumstance.

During the break, too, I was thinking about states of being. Freud wrote about moods playing a big role in his creativity, a recurrent emphasis in the Freud–Fliess letters. Mood gives rise to thought, image, narrative, dance, gesture. A lot comes up in us that we say no to. If a scary image or thought comes, we can comfort ourselves by saying, it's just imaginary. It's not real, it's just a thought. But imagination helps create real states of mind, amazing states of mind.

One amazing power is the capacity to null, nullify, to n-o-t rather than k-n-o-t.

There's an emphasis in mysticism on nullification of the self. A paradoxical capacity. It seems to be one pole of a double capacity: to nullify, affirm. Affirm self, nullify self. Like pulse beats, heartbeats: yes/no, self/no-self, true/false, right/wrong.

Rabbi Schneerson talks about nullification to such an extreme that he feels God, at this moment, is creating you and the world out of nothing. Every moment. And if God, even for a milli-instant, stopped creating the world out of nothing, there would be no world, no you: an amazing and beautiful image of ultimate dependence on a mysterious not-you that creates you out of nothing.

We are made of so many processes it is impossible to find a definitive beginning. You can say this element or tendency is more important than that, or even assign primacy to one over another, but you are selecting out of a larger pool, probably made of many unknowns. This is so even with your own history. As much as you know about yourself, there is more that eludes knowing. In the end, you have to drop your jaw and say, it's a mystery. I'm a mystery! And if I go with Rabbi Shneerson, perhaps awe that God is creating me this moment out of nothing. Nothing is part of us, part of what makes us up, our building material. Another binary: nothing–someone, am–am not. Bion says that a thing can only be if it is and is not at the same time. We are gifted with double capacities, to be and not to be, null and affirm, qualities that are part of persistence and plasticity.

Spiritual systems talk about no-form. Chuang-Tzu writes that a hidden One has identity but no form. Kabbalah—*Ein Sof*. Buddhism— emptiness is form, form emptiness. We are gifted with so many possible states, multiplicities of experience. Even qualities of nothing vary, change in valence, for example, nothings experienced along positive–negative, creative–destructive continua.

*   *   *

Bion's grid (Figure 2; Bion, 1989; Eigen, 2012a, 2013) is rooted in the unknown. One can look at the grid as a way of charting growth of experience from less to more known. Both the grid and the *sephirot* begin with the unknown. For the latter, *Ein Sof*, unknown, unpresentable, unimaginable, unspeakable reality, beyond anything nameable (including what we call reality). A kinship with poetry evoking what cannot be said, poetry of the unspeakable.

The *sephirot* begin with ineffable mystery. A lot goes on before reaching the *sephirot*, but, once reached, the *sephirot* seem to grow from top down, a vertical system (see Eigen, 1986, for a critique of the vertical). Yet, the interaction within the system has a lot of flow. Each *sephira* has infinities of *sephirot*. All *sephirot* are in each other in infinities of possible ways.

Bion's grid looks more like a graph, with vertical and horizontal elements, a mathematical feel. The *sephirot*, like a tree with branches, also has vertical–horizontal flows. If you focus on the categories in Bion's grid, you can begin to see emergence and growth of experience. Bion warns us not to be confined by his categories. More can be added. He explicitly mentioned a need to add more sub-categories to C (dream-thoughts, dreams, myths). Other categories or subcategories can be added as needed, perhaps as awareness of growth of experience grows. He even suggests making your own grid, useful for your personality and perception (Bion, 1989, 1997).

The grid looks very rigid, but is not as rigid as you might think. You might say Bion tries to develop a mental instrument to glimpse the beginning and growth of thought (or feeling, possibly even sensation), the beginning and growth of experience: the grid as a kind of mental intrument or aid, akin to a telescope for seeing astronomical bodies.

He begins by positing something unobserved, beta elements, at the top of the vertical column. One could talk a long time about why he

THE GRID

	Definitory Hypotheses	ψ	Notation	Attention	Inquiry	Action	
	1	2	3	4	5	6	. . . n
A β-elements	A1	A2				A6	
B α-elements	B1	B2	B3	B4	B5	B6	. . . Bn
C Dream Thoughts Dreams, Myths	C1	C2	C3	C4	C5	C6	. . . Cn
D Pre-conception	D1	D2	D3	D4	D5	D6	. . . Dn
E Conception	E1	E2	E3	E4	E5	E6	. . . En
F Concept	F1	F2	F3	F4	F5	F6	. . . Fn
G Scientific Deductive system		G2					
H Algebraic Calculus							

Figure 2.   Bion's Grid.

begins with A (Beta-elements) rather than B (Alpha-elements), rather than the other way around, since it takes some alpha work to know or experience or sense or posit beta work. Sometimes I tend to look at beta-elements as raw impacts sensed by experience, often catastrophic impacts, trauma globs. Something hits and we may try to process it. Something like getting bitten by an insect without knowing it, discovering the fact through a pressing itch. Or not knowing you have been hit by a bullet until discovering the wound, possibly by its effects on functioning and rising pain. Bion emphasises catastrophic impacts because he hones in on psychotic processes in human life. But he associates catastrophe with the birth of consciousnes as well, and perhaps with psychic birth (conscious and unconscious). The impact of beta need not, I suspect, be limited to trauma. A range of impacts is likely, registering at some point along a pleasure–pain continuum and ineffable dimensions as well. Wordsworth's "Prelude", for example, channels ineffable experience through moving poetry. Chapter Four of *The Psychotic Core* (Eigen, 1986) sketches possible moments of psychic flow through a sweep of feeling in early infancy.

Bion begins with beta elements and says, I have never seen one. I do not know what it is. It is not anything I have seen in reality but in case it shows up, I have a category for it. He creates varying descriptions of it. Let's use something of a physical analogy for the moment. Let's make believe your body is animate (laughter). One of the big themes in British psychoanalysis, shared by Winnicott and Bion, is how we de-animate ourselves. For Bion we begin animate—more, everything seems animated. How do we tone down, dampen, kill off the animate quality of experience over time? Through natural developmental processes and overly traumatic developmental processes.

Let's say a beta element builds pressure to the point where it begins to obtrude on our pan-animate beings. To some extent, impact on animate sensitivity can be excruciating. How much of an impact can be tolerated before our psycho-organism seeks means of escape? How welcoming can our systems be to an impinging beta element, or even one that merely knocks on our door? Do we seek both to process and shut it out at the same time, let it in in handleable doses? As we develop, in varying contexts, a thought seeking a thinker, or - feeling seeking a feeler, or sensation seeking a senser can be a raw beta element needing psychic work and hospitality. Freud writes of impinging stimuli and resulting sensations developing the cerebral cortex as a protective shield fostering growing awareness of reality. Both functions together: a degree of protection from impact so that impact can be assessed (e.g., danger/non-danger). Freud notes stimulation itself can be dangerous, a first trauma being stimulus and emotional flooding.

Even in the womb, and, some might say, before the womb (in Kabbalah, one hears the soul shriek in its descent towards the womb), the foetus might feel pressures of different kinds. The optic pits might light up because of pressures on it. If so, seeing light begins early—light in darkness, a virtually omnipresent image in many contexts and levels. Or changes in the body might scare you, sudden magnification of sound, shifting pressures of blood flowing in one's head (a panicky fear in psychosis), or a baby or young child frightened by changes in blood pressure without having a frame of reference for what is happening. Winnicott describes somatic-feeling agonies akin to being dropped off a cliff linked to sudden change in states. Freud wrote about early chaotic sensory flows shaped into relative unities with time. We have worlds of background pressures without thought, words, or cognitive frames that can have an impact on thinking, or how we hold our bodies, or how our bodies hold us. Unknown pressures and waves that impact on the field of experience. Even changes in state might feel chaotic and threatening, one state disrupting another. We might be experiencing hovering beta elements awaiting, evoking need of somato-psychic work.

What we call chaotic might undergo spontaneous organisation. Much of our perceptual world spontaneously organises itelf into seamless fields of awareness. If we stay with a chaotic state long enough, it tends to become organised. Alpha function can play a role in organising raw impacts and learning from experience. Alpha work can be creative and/or pedestrian. It plays a role in developing narratives about raw emotional pressures and impacts, like dreams and myths. It plays a role in storing experiencing and readying it for use. I suspect alpha work is part of our innate beginnings, or interweaving of beta–alpha elements could not occur. Interweaving capacities that are needed to stimulate and sustain the life form we are.

Bion notes that important as alpha function is in the process of psychic digestion and creation, it also produces narrative organisations that trap us. We may feel creative joy, but our products can also make us feel claustraphobic. In such a scenario, a little chaos is a relief rather than persecutory. Bion envisions a back and forth between chaos or fragmentation and organisation. In a way, we feel a need to break through our capacities, as if our windows on experience feel limiting. The very capacities that organise us via alpha function become menacing beta elements tugging at the pillars of our temples.

I have used the words background pressures to give a sense of beta impact, but there may be no language that works well enough. Bion was driven to postulate Greek letters for unknown processes that may or may not exist. If his work begins to sound a little kabbalistic, it is. There are many affinities (Eigen, 2012a, 2013). Both develop languages to express work of unknown forces. We try to find/create language that opens experiencing as best we can.

In many passages, Bion associates beta elements with sensation, partly in analogy with the Greek *hyle*, basic raw material to develop. The word sensation is one of those evocative words that span a range of dimensions. Most often, it is associated with bodily sensation, pleasure, pain, the five senses. But it also can refer to "common sense", which Bion says cannot be taken for granted. In psychosis, for example, the various senses might work against each other rather than with each other. We might find ourselves conlicted between what different senses offer. There are also ineffable "sensations", for some, a God sensation. Or sensing akin to intuition. Erotic sensations can be ineffable—erotic infinities (Eigen, 2006). If beta elements are associated with sensation, possible domains they touch expand like an accordion with unending keys.

Bion says he does not mean the same thing as sense that most psychologists mean. What sorts of sensation stir us at the beginnings of psychic life? Only pain and pleasure, or also horror and bliss? Hosts of affect sensations, some more boundless than others? Passing and forever sensations? What can it mean in the Bible, the Lord of Hosts? Not just the literal meaning (is there such a thing as a literal *meaning*?) usually given, but perhaps also hosts of experiences. One sense, at the level of beta, is sensation infinities. Immaterial sensations that cannot be located anywhere, such as a sense of the eerie or beatific. B(eta) for beginning. Unknown beginnings of psychic life. Alpha and beta—as with biblical figures or Freud's depiction of emotions—reversal is often the rule.

Associating beta with psychic beginnings can also be misleading, considering all the unknowable proesses at work off the grid that enable something to reach grid expression, the latter including beta elements. The off the grid unknown might have parallels with unknowable supernal processes giving rise to the creative *sephirot*, mediating birth of world and human functioning.

Bion, also, postulated a minus grid, grid processes working in reverse. In parallel fashion, one can imagine minus *sephirot*, the *sephirot* Tree of Life working in reverse. Positive and negative grids, positive and negative trees of life. Processes that undo themselves, moving towards zero, going into zero, beyond zero, gone, very gone. Destructive grids, destructive trees of life. Bion wrote of a destructive force that goes on destroying after everything is destroyed, feeding off destruction, tending towards pure destruction. Double tendencies: building, undoing building. Freud's life drive building unities, the death drive dismantling.

There are people who are caught between building and not letting anything build. Some people cannot begin, some can begin but cannot bring a project to fruition. Unable to begin, unable to end. And so many with problems in the middle. Recently, I have been meeting more and more young people who cannot finish college. They stay up all night on the computer but cannot organise the means–end behaviour that would accomplish the goal of going from beginning to end. They can write all night with Internet friends they might never meet in person, but cannot organise the acts needed to hand in a course paper. It is as if the timeless, boundless computer world takes the place of exertion in time and the demands and pressures of time.

* * *

Between Passover and Shavuos—leaving Egypt and receiving the Ten Comandments on Mount Sinai—are fifty days. On each of those days, one corrects another personal or group fault, so that by the time Moses receives the *Torah*, the children of Israel have raised themselves to a point more suitable for living *Torah*. It is said that while slaves in Egypt, they sunk to the forty-ninth level of depravity. Had they sunk one more level, even God could not redeem them. But, in the fifty days between leaving and receiving, they made up a lot of ground. Ground, to be sure, often shaky, with much back-tracking. A story that includes pessismism but sides with optimism. It expresses a basic pattern of going through the worst or nearly worst and becoming something better.

A lot of strife goes into a moment of destiny. It is said the Ten Commandments are inscribed in every Jewish heart. Even at the minus forty-ninth level of defilement, enough godly elements remained so that *Torah* inscription could take place. Let's imagine that hate of God competed with love of God, or perhaps not caring about God at all competed with an innate devotional tendency. At the minus forty-ninth level, enough love remained for *Torah* meeting to occur or, at least, be envisioned as something to strive for. One might say, that no matter what the Hebrews did, they could not rid themselves of love of God.

This is, of course, a very parochial story. Today, we can see in it archetypal elements and apply it to humanity more broadly. It expresses basic affective patterns, emotions we experience and work with. Moments of life we go through.

The idea of going through what cannot be gone through resonates with aspects of psychoanalysis.

* * *

The idea/reality expressed by the "z dimension" is particularly challenging, not just for psychoanalysis. The term "z dimension" is something I drew from a Winnicott passage and amplified for broader use. Winnicott wrote of mother separating from baby x amount of time, mother comes back, baby is all right. Mother separates from baby longer, y amount of time, more travail when she comes back, but there is resilience and things are good enough. Mother is away z time and the baby suffers permanent damage. To be permanently damaged does not necessarily mean that you are only damaged. But you feel it and know it is part of you. You may have creative capacities that meet the damage, that might even be stimulated by damage. You might have social capacities or compensatory capacities that make life worthwhile. But there is also an inner sense of something wrong (Eigen, 2009).

Freud wrote about permanent alterations in personality for the worse in "Analysis terminable and interminable" (1937). Something happened to your capacity to change, to go through states. Something off in the rhythm of the psyche. Bion (1994), too, notes that in the psychotic attitude, capacity to go back and forth between states in fruitful ways is wounded. Balint (1992) touches this in writing of "malignant regressions", regressions that militate against rather than promote recovery. He contrasts states one cannot do much about with benevolent regression, which leads to healing and new beginnings.

My feeling throughout my career, over fifty years, has been what can we do with those who do not get better, with those we cannot seem to help. Can we help some more of the "unhelpables"? It is great to help people who respond to help, someone who seems to have resources to make use of what therapy offers—I'm all for that. At the same time, I am intensely interested in people who hit or present a wall. Perhaps I gravitate towards this beause there are parts of me that cannot be helped. That is what Bion tried to work with in the hope of someday being able to access emotional experience in such a way "to hasten the day when what is perhaps the most distressing malady a patient and family have to endure will be classed as 'curable'" (1994, p. 261).

I think Winnicott, too, worked at the edge of the possible. He had a special interest in people who did not feel real and sought ways in therapy to touch this. To touch the untouchable, working in the z dimension, that part of the self that suffered "permanent" alteration. To reach the unreachable, psychosis to psychosis (Eigen, 2009).

The term z dimension raises many questions. If the z dimension is precisely what cannot be worked with, how can we work with it? Perhaps it is more apt to say, it cannot be worked with now. Or has not been worked with in a reliably successful way. Macbeth asks, "Canst though not minister to a mind diseased?" The doctor answers, that only the patient herself can do this. In a talk, Bion answered with something like, "Not now. But come back in two hundred years and we'll see."

I have seen openings in aspects of the z dimension in my lifetime. When I first started seeing patients in the 1960s, there was a buzz about a newish category called "borderline psychosis": people who might react in psychotic-like ways, go in and out of psychotic states, but do not have to be hospitalised. They may function in crippled ways, but tend to function or have areas of functioning and, in one way or another, go on with life. They learn to put up with a lot of suffering.

I remember being hit like a bomb by my first "borderline", a woman with acute sensitivity to emotional pain that triggered chaotic storms she could not manage. Yet, she was able to relay what was happening as it was happening, moment to moment, blow by blow accounts of the raging winds within. At times, I felt I was hearing passages from a Shakespeare play. Right or wrong, I could not but admire her exceptional sensitivity and heightened ability to express it. For the patient, living with it on a day-to-day basis was another matter.

At the time, there were not a lot of therapists who could work well with so-called "borderlines". The acute, chaotic responses to emotional pain could be paralysing, the intensity of anger hard to bear. Borderline anger as a response to frustration became "famous" among clinicians. Individuals went from therapist to therapist. A literature about such cases burgeoned. Interest and controversies ensued. On a gut, clinical level, little by little, inroads were made.

As time went on, more therapists became more comfortable and able to work with this sub-group. Why? I think of a particular mother bird who needs the baby bird to peck her in a particular spot in order for her mothering impulse to kick into gear. I think what partly happened was the borderline's anger pecked the therapy field until the response systems needed began to develop. I will not say the work is easy—it is challenging and often labile. But my sense is that many of us now can work with people that eluded help some decades earlier. This is not just a matter of intellectual knowledge, but growth in emotional responsiveness as well. Whether or not we can help Lady Macbeth in two hundred years remains to be seen. And we do not know what kind of growth is needed or possible for the help Bion envisions for the most severely distressed. Yet, many of us are compelled, in the hope that the capacities needed to make a difference find ways. Even today, if a Daniel Paul Schreber (2000) comes into our office and speaks of "soul murder", we have little trouble sensing what he means, something unlikely one hundred years ago. But whether or not we can help this particular individual is not known until we try.

Perhaps what I am trying to say is that work with people who "cannot be worked with" enabled me to begin contacting aspects of myself that cannot be worked with in more meaningful ways. The acute sensitivity and rage of the borderline, the "soul murder" of psychosis, gives me a language for aspects of myself that sometimes whisper in the crevices, but more often scream from the core.

* * *

I would like to offer a few more notes on z dimension. Perhaps there are z aspects that can be worked with and z aspects that cannot, like plus and minus grid or *sephirot*, plus and minus z dimensions, z plus and minus infinities. In some cases, sludge, dead weights, inert but powerfully lurking densities, in others, high voltage that becomes higher the nearer one gets.

I am thinking more on the notion that the Hebrews reached the minus forty-ninth level of spiritual deterioration while slaves in Egypt, and had they reached the fiftieth they would be unhelpable. In my concept of the z dimension, there could be no unhelpable level beyond possibility of trying to help. It might not be possible to help, but it is possible to make an attempt. Persistent or intermittent attempts can enable helping capacity to develop over time, perhaps not noticeable for long periods, but one cannot conclude definitively that nothing is happening or will happen. A little like a person in a coma who might or might not revive, life may be going on out of sight.

Once we speak of the Hebrews as slaves in Egypt (for certain rabbis, Egypt in the Bible story represents materialism), we are caught in a master–slave binary. There are ways that many of us undergo a slave stage in life. Much is given up, but much is learnt working hard for others. One learning can be the value of working hard, which can spread to include oneself and humanity, spread to include creative work, the experience of creativity, the value of hard, creative labour. To use oneself with all one has, all one's might, is a value in itself.

To be a master is to be a slave once removed. One remains a slave to the idea of master, for example, a power addict. Neither slave nor master represents psychic freedom. As long as the z dimension exists, slavery exists. If z partly represents negative beta elements, raw material for further work is inexhaustible.

Trying and not trying make up another binary, rich with possibilities. There might come a point where giving up makes more sense than trying, although, given the kind of beings we are, there is no reason why both processes cannot go on at the same time. Trying as one tendency, giving up another, both working together. There is the giving up of defeat. There is also creative inaction, the cessation of non-action, letting Tao work. A giving up that is more a letting go, even a trust, a faith, at times faith conjoined with loss of faith.

*   *   *

I associated the z dimension with beta elements. Bion says he has never seen a beta element, but posits it in case one shows up. Beta elements can become frozen or be envisioned as agglutinated bizarre masses that cement caesuras. Or they can represent raw impacts or pressures needing processing. They can form part of the psi-barrier in column two of the grid, partly made up of lies that act as a contact barrier between unconscious and conscious processes. Then again, beta elements can make themselves known as physical pains, a neck-ache or backache exerting somatic pressure aching for psychic work. I have heard psychotic individuals express fright over whirring sensations in their brains. One person said, "If only you can reassure me that my brain isn't getting damaged, I can go through this." He meant crackling, whirring tensions taken as signs that his brain was in physical jeapordy. One might regard these sensations as beta elements signalling catastrophe in progress, lacking capacity to locate the latter. Beta elements can have various functions in psychic life, feeding, stimulating, blocking, or even destroying, processing. There may be benefit in thinking of positive and negative beta elements depending on how they function in a given context, similar to positive–negative grid, *sephirot*, and z functions.

A job of alpha function is to work on beta elements, whatever they are. Bion uses the term, "whatever it is" a number of times. I like Bion's open-ended use of this phrase and like him saying "something's happening", something is going on, without being able to say what it is. For me, this is true to clinical experience. You may sense something happening without being able to say what it is. At times, it is better not to try to name it prematurely, let it keep happening. There is no better way to kill an elusive movement than to say, this is what it is, and feel right about it. You might be sensing a few strands of complex networks that exceed your grasp. Pinning them down might mislead, mis-shape, give them meaning that truncates their movement. Alpha work can go on without words. For example, incipient alpha processing of catastrophic beta globs can go on in dreams. At the end of his book, *Second Thoughts* (1984), Bion goes over some of the dream interpretations he gave in earlier papers, pointing out which remarks stopped the flow of the dream and which enabled dreamwork to continue. A session that stops dreaming feels different from one that supports dream experience. Bion felt that dreamwork goes on twenty-four hours a day and it makes a difference whether it is stillborn or adds to psychic birth.

Bion associates alpha elements with storing and digesting experience, working with experience. He writes of damaged alpha function, which has some kinship with damaged primary process. Much experience is aborted or undergoes deformation, in so far as alpha function is damaged. It is like having something wrong with your digestive system, in this case emotional digestion, so that you might be living in chronic states of pychic indigestion (Eigen, 2001b).

I see beta and alpha as interweaving. Often, they are presented as opposed. I feel they are interwoven not just in the sense of beta feeding alpha impacts for storage and digestion, but more thoroughly interwoven, so that you do not have one without the other. They permeate each other. It might be too extreme to say that wherever there is beta, alpha is nibbling. Perhaps not quite right to say that beta carries packets or pockets of alpha potential within it. I have not found the words to express what I sense, but the former two inadequate statements suggest a closeness, symbiosis. Beta needs alpha, alpha needs beta. Where beta is, processing begins, we try to work with it, turn it this way and that, taste it, feel it, a kind of beta farm in which psychic life grows.

Yes, they can become antagonists, beta shields turned destructive. And, at times, alpha grows through adversarial relationships. But one can also envision beta as food for alpha, psychic life stretching, learning, becoming bit by bit. A beta headache or heartache, an alpha headache or heartache, an alphabeta ache, as one suffers the growth of processing. Muted aches that translate into longings, or longings that translate into muted aches.

It might be an over-zealous psychoanalyst who thinks breaking a blood vessel might have something to do with anger. But Marion Milner is one such "zealot" (2012). Near the end of her life, in her nineties, she links a burst blood vessel in her left eye with "my own secretly rebellious Satanic self that might have caused this bursting". She goes on to say that medical experts might link the burst with shifts in blood pressure.

> But what about anger? Doesn't ordinary speech say "I was so angry I could have burst a blood vessel" . . . it could be that what had sparked off my eye burst was a terror that a split-off and angrily rebellious part of myself would emerge with disastrous results. But why an eye burst? Could it be that a bit of me felt that to burst an eye blood vessel, which happens silently, is better than to burst out with Satanic rebellious speech? (p. 251)

In the context of our present discussion, Milner's broken blood vessel could be a beta–alpha amalgam or condensation, in which psyche speaks silently. In a still deeper vein, it might be that some-thing is exerting pressure to be known, a feeling seeking a feeler, a thought in search of a thinker, a sensation seeking a senser, beta aspects needing alpha, more alpha, or alpha in another vein. Or, perhaps, beta and alpha in search of each other.

Another way of putting such a state of affairs is that something has broken through the beta screen or stream, a broken blood vessel has entered awareness, and alpha picks up the ball and runs with it. While we cannot say what is true or false in definitive ways, we can legiti-mately conjecture that Milner's conjectures, using her vessel burst as stimulus, are psychically enriching. Her feeling–thought processes turn around the vessel, as if viewing a Rodin sculpture in progress. It feels like this, looks like this . . . Meanwhile, psyche grows richer, bit by bit. A sense of possibility grows, awareness expands, becomes fuller, something thaws further.

Bion's work on beta-alpha and, to an extent, Milner's exploration, hint how much psychic life is out of awareness. Our whole circulatory system is out of awareness. However, an infant might experience dread when blood flow in the brain changes; sensations without a frame of reference can frighten. For example, my psychotic patient, who experiences fear when feeling what he takes to be damaging brain tensions. Shifts in blood flow, pressures, digestive and respira-tory sensations, to name a few, might yield sensings that undergo animation. One goes back and forth between a threatening body and a pleasure body, or both inextricably fused. The body itself can be animated and seem a foreign being outside or within me, demonic or divine.

A language of aches and pains and pleasures. Beta becoming a primitive alpha element in the pain itself. An ache trying to let you know something about its existence. An ache trying to let you know something about your existence. The background unknown speaking to you. Often, beta is associated with sensation, but here Bion touches alpha sensation, primitive forms of somatopsychic communication. In a way, Bion is saying be grateful for a headache/heartache or a nightmare that scares you half to death. You might be trying to com-municate with yourself. This does not mean you should not see a doctor about a persistent or unusual pain, see if you have a brain tumor or something wrong with your digestive system. But it might be a beta element trying to say hello, or an alpha ache trying to get your attention. "Hey! I'm here! There's a lot more to you than you know." The whole background of your existence and messages about the state of your life. Perhaps you can begin seeking contact with what is seeking you by meditating on the taste of your existence, how it feels to be you throughout a day.

*   *   *

It is tempting to say that Bion's grid bears resemblance to the *sephirot* upside down. Rather than starting with higher thought and working its way down throgh emotion and action, as the *sephirot* do, Bion starts with elusive impacts and pressures that gradually emerge as image, feeling, thought on the vertical axis, and move through a series of emergent steps towards attention, enquiry, and action on the horizontal axis. Chapters could be written about each category. The vertical axis is perhaps easier to understand at a glance, since a movement towards greater abstraction seems obvious. It is a Bion teaching, however, that no matter how great the abstraction, something of the particular remains. The play of beta elements continues throughout the range of the psyche or mind. Alpha is always working with beta at every level. I experience the two as interpenetrating. One might see beta as more obdurate, impermeable, and, in many circumstances, that might be so. But as I once heard a poet, Elizabeth Sewell, say, even a rock is permeable. Psychic work involves difference with permeability.

The horizontal axis appears to be more difficult. Here is one possible sketch, just for starters. Let's say that an impact gives rise to some obscure, implicit "conjecture", "hunch" of what the pressure is. A felt sense of what is happening before it reaches a point where I might say, anger, I am angry, or anger is attacking me, or knocking on my door. The second horizontal category, the psi function, might build upon the "hunch", slow conscious–unconscious input–output, so that a selection towards meaning can be made from the swarming abyss. Bion sometimes calls column two "lies", which suggests a slant on the pressure or impact (beta) is now circling the impact, enclosing it with psychic work, which eventuates in meaning and action. Lies, because all psychic work is selective, biased, perhaps organised by tropisms, tensions of tendencies. Beta objects become known to us, in part, by the way we organise them. We select from beta impacts bits of the impact spectrum and we select and rework them in specific ways. In a way, psychic work is work with hunches, intimations.

Notation (column 3) continues this process. How do we make internal notations to ourselves? An obscure psychic sensing, noting this feels that way, that feels this way; a semi-unconscious array of sensings of psychical qualities. We have only glimpses of processes that go on without words or images, although images and words eventually grow from it. We clothe raw impacts with emergent processes.

At some point, we are able to pay attention to emergent processes that mediate sensation, feeling, thought, action. We can begin to focus on beta fields permeated with alpha work, semi-organised by dreamwork and mythic narratives, seeds feeding imaginative reflection and enquiry. Some minimal balance or compensation for inevitable biases of psychic organisation is attempted through attention and enquiry. With the latter, we have some chance of looking at psychic perturbations from a variety of perspectives, turning them this or that way, again, like seeing a Rodin sculpture from many angles. This process can be slow or fast. It can work to mitigate impulsiveness or justify it. One can sit with action urges and see something about what goes into them and one can explore components of mental processes, each of the grid categories, each of the *sephirot*. We will not rid ourselves of our makeup but, one hopes, learn to work with it a little better, become better partners with our capacities. At the same time, all our studies of "higher" or "lower" end capacities have roots in the vast unknown, supernal and subtending. Our pleasure and pride in exercising our capacities must take place within a greater horizon of humility.

*   *   *

Very often, I hear the phrase, "It feels right". A person might use such a feeling or phrase to justify a course of action or way of looking at a situation, another person, and oneself. It is hard to get used to the idea that because it feels right does not mean it *is* right, or even if right is relevant for the matter at hand at all. The more I see, the more I become sensitive to the possibility that a sense of being right can be a signal that something destructive might be around the corner. A sense of being right has been used to justify going to war, a tendency that can work on many levels, personal, familial, within and between groups. We seem addicted to feeling right, as if that gives us the right to assert our position, even supremacy, over others (who are less right or wrong; Eigen, 2002).

A concept may organise aspects of the unknowable. Perhaps an ancient Greek might feel a thought came to him, whereas we tend to feel it as my thought, *I* think. We are invested in concepts that spontaenously organise aspects of experience. To some extent, over time, we might mistake a concept for an experience it tries to organise in certain ways. We even invest it with own-ership. My thought or way of thinking *vs.* yours. Ownership is rooted very deep psychically, not only in terms of territory and possessions but mental, psychical, spiritual objects as well: my God *vs.* yours, thou shalt have no other gods before me, I am a possessive God.

I remember years of arguments about right and wrong psychoanalytic interpretations, and how you can tell a correct one by the flow of a patient's associations. This can get pretty complicated. One can envision being right, yet cruel with destructive effects, or wrong, but kind with helpful consequences. In time, for some of us at least, right and wrong became less important than something else harder to put into words. Sometimes, a beautiful or rich "interpretation", gesture, or remark gives rise to something decent or good.

There were times when I was younger that I made some interpretations that apparently had good consequences. I put it this way because, as important as some remarks can be—and some can come as revelations that open new possibilities, I tend to place more on atmospheric conditions over time. But here is one moment, embedded in a larger relationship, that was telling. A woman spoke of headaches, which brought to mind something I learnt years before: head–father, stomach–mother. I do not know if this little formula holds up. I have never investigated it. But it came to me as I was listening and I wondered if it would have any value. So I asked my patient to say more about her father. She went into lengthy descriptions of good and bad times together, what she loved about him and what was missing. By the time she stopped speaking, her headache had gone away. Did she talk her headache away? Was it my interest, the richness of her communication? Would her headache have left if she had immersed herself in another topic? Was immersion more the key than specific content? And what did we miss by my creating this focus? What might have happened had I not organised it by a formula that came to me from the past? Did I steal a bucket of water from a larger well? It seemed to work, but at unknown cost. Did God plant an alpha or beta object in her head for other purposes? Something happened against a backdrop of a larger unknown. In Kabbalah, emphasis is on the great Unknown above that permeates all. Perhaps Bion emphasises a great unknown below as well, unknown promptings that make their way through our various organising capacities, including sensation, feeling, emotion, thought, intuition. In both instances, the infinite unnown remains a permanent background for foreground knowing.

*   *   *

Row C, Dream Thoughts, Dreams, Myth, plays a special role in Bion's work. He feels an analyst should have at her/his disposal a reservoir of myths to draw on as a situation needs. Myths that are meaningful to the analyst's life, so that they have a ring of realness, myths emotionally real for the analyst that can be used as a lens to illuminate aspects of the patient's psyche. The kind of "objectivity" used in analysis is very subjective, or has a subjective component. The latter is not simply a perennial source of distortion (it is) but also part of intuitive conviction that opens gates. Bion suggests the analyst free associate repeatedly to aspects of mythic narratives and images to keep intuition/alpha function in good repair.

He also feels that primal alpha–beta work (Rows A and B) often gives rise to images which act as vehicles to store experience. Images can act as ideograms packed with potential meaning awaiting unpacking, unravelling, creative elaboration. Images may condense perceptual memories of emotional significance or add something elusive and new. In *Icon and Idea* (1965), Herbert Read argues that image is often two hundred years ahead of idea.

A distinction as well as a link can be made between dream and myth, the former private the latter public, although crossover happens. Let's say impact happens. As comic books say, "Pow!", "Bang!" Perhaps a jolt, something touches, rocks, sends shivers. Sweet or sour impacts. Something hits, but you may not know what, like a bullet going through you that you discover moments later. For present communication, let's say impact through alpha work translates into image. It is temping to identify image with alpha function. They are closely related. Yet, Bion lets us know that alpha is the broader function and much less is known about it. Image is more intact, coherent, formed. Alpha is more an invisible forming function, not confined to one kind of product.

In "A little psyche music", a chapter in *The Sensitive Self* (2004), I write about alpha dancing or an alpha baseball catch in comparison with a beta moment. Alpha function is already at work in wordless, imageless dance, although one might say that dance itself is imagistic. One could also say that the muscular, sensorial, proprioceptive, kinaesthetic feel of the body propels dance. Our body is an affective, imaginative body. A line of association could be drawn starting with felt perceptual significance, body sensing, and affective propulsion or efflorescence (whether joy, conciliation, propitiation, terror, anger, hope) giving rise to image giving rise to "thought". However, I take such lines lightly, as many lines can be drawn.

A speciality of Bion is exploring psychosis, or psychotic attitudes and states. He writes of the importance of catastrophic impacts. A beta moment might embody and transmit an impact translated as flooding (one of Freud's terms for primal trauma) or nameless dread. Dreams of getting killed, forced entry (including physical penetration), other invasions, loss or isolation give specificity to free-floating catastrophe (Eigen, 2005). Catastrophic impacts and dreads not only effect psychic contents and structure, but also a sense of psychic space, which can so expand that one does not feel oneself as living or real, or shrink to the point of suffocation, or deform so that one feels deformed just by being alive.

It is important to note that Bion does not limit catastrophe to psychosis. It can be part of creativity as well. He depicts both the onset of psychosis and consciousness in general as a kind of big bang that can go either or both ways (Eigen, 1998). He wonders about a state that can turn into psychosis or creativity or both, but does not tell us what this state might be, or, rather, tells us in many ways but leaves it open. In trying to communicate with students, I sometimes call it a stem cell state, which can take on different forms and functions depending on context and conditions.

Perhaps pressure from unknown beta elements becomes painful (beta, alpha) and the pain, among other things, translates into dream. A dream might be an attempt to call attention to bits of catastrophic realities. Many dreams are scary, if not nightmares, and one often wakes up before the feared happening quite occurs. Often hints or beginnings of catastrophic happenings jar one awake. Many dreams abort the affective reality they try to express, as it appears the intensity of affect can be too much for the dreamwork. Bion introduces the notion that trying to dream what cannot be dreamt, a state of affairs too frightening for dreaming to handle, might damage dreamwork itself. In so far as alpha is working as part of dreaming, trying to store, express, and process experience, it can become damaged by the experience it tries to work with. Mythic warnings against seeing God or Medusa lest you die apply to dreamwork biting off more than it can chew. In psychic work, dosing toxicity and danger is important.

Why is there so close a connection between psychosis and creativity? One reason, I suspect, is that many psychoses can only be worked with creatively. In some cases, psychosis is aborted creativity, creativity gone wrong. Something in the psychotic individual reverberates to creative responses in the other, whether the latter are effective or not. Creativity enlivens, brings dead songbirds to life. There are many kinds of psychosis (Eigen, 1986), some more burnt out, habituated downwards, some cinders still smouldering, some strangulated aliveness waiting for resuscitation. Some patients can meet you half way, some can hardly let a breath of life stir out of fear that it, too, will be killed or deformed, and some habitually stay in adaptations that keep one alive in narrow channels. There are many other possibilities, including variations on high–low intensity spectrums.

While in New York, I heard Bion say that if you (the analyst) are not in Row C, in touch with dreaming processes, you are not in the session. Higher level thought might be good between sessions, but in the session itself you dip into dreamwork. You co-participate in dreaming. It is unlikely that it is either/or, since we move back and forth through levels, now closer to dream, now closer to conceptual thought. I was going to write closer to conception, but realised that dreamwork is involved in conception, birthing the psyche. One of the virtues in Bion's writing is one feels he is in contact with processes he describes, observes the psychotic attitude within unfolding, in it and out of it at the same time. In this, he models a capacity the patient needs more of: to be in touch with the states that dominate and imprison, while developing freedom enough to explore them, maintaining contact with the compacted life they contain while lessening their destructiveness.

Bion uses the couple, omnipotence–helplessness, as an example of concepts that mask elusive wordless dimensions. We think we know what we mean by these words, their reference to being all powerful or powerless. For example, an omnipotent God, a helpless baby. But what psychic work does framing experience this way mask? Many micro-processes are at work in framing an idea of omnipotence–helplessness that are lost in these global terms. The global idea gives one a handle, a feeling one knows what one is talking about, while many psychic fish swim through the net.

Bion writes several times of the Great Death Pit of Ur, where biblical Abraham came from, now modern Iraq. Members of the court were buried alive with the dead king or queen (although workers and servants might have been killed beforehand, then dressed in finery), with the help of a drug or poison and perhaps the thought of a better life. One thinks of modern phenomena like Jonestown: mass religious suicide.

In *Emotional Storm* (Eigen, 2005), there is a chapter on the urge to kill oneself, an urge that reaches deep. Staying awake and in life has difficulties. One imagines there is no pain in death, although Hamlet was not so sure. Clifford Scott (1975) wrote of a conflict between the urge to stay awake and the compulsion to go to sleep. There is a pull towards states of dark night. It is not just the newborn infant that needs to rest from awakeness. One imagines dream life embodies this double tendency, a pull towards dreamless void and heightened awareness.

The Death Pit of Ur fascinated Bion, in part because it brought out the mystery of a religious force that works in so many ways, even to the point of convincing people to die as part of a ritual or communal idea. He suspected facile, if important, terms such as omnipotence blur the work of a force that has a hold on our psyche and exerts mysterious influence on our lives. A phrase such as "has a hold on our psyche" suggests something external to us having a hold on us, whereas the problem is deeper, in as much as our psyche is partly constituted by this force and is interwoven with it. It is not something extrinsic, but intrinsic.

When Bion was in New York, the only analyst who worked on this continent that he mentioned was Theodore Reik. He expressed his liking of Reik's writing on surprise. I would like to mention another of Reik's works, as it adds an extra bit of colour to the domain we are beginning to touch. He saw accidents, like hitting your head while putting something in the boot of a car, as a compromise between life and death instincts. Instead of killing yourself, you merely injure yourself, in this case not catastrophically (although the latter occurs all too frequently).

The above are some of the ways one gets a hint of the many states that mix a need for loss of consciousness, sleep, death, and spectrums of varied states of awareness. The more one reads Kabbalah and psychoanalysis, the more one appreciates their speculative imagination. Bion speaks of the importance of giving imagination free reign, akin to Freud writing of letting the horse lead the rider, following the lead of the creative unconscious. Bion also speaks of following phases of speculative imagination with the work of speculative reason. You can always make up images and reasons. Reasons are associated with science—one might say, the science of images or imaginings. Speculative reason is a creative activity in itself. After you let imaginings and reasonings come, you can think about them, akin to Wordsworth's definition of poetry as emotion recollected in tranquillity.

In my sessions with Bion, he often sided with the realness of frightening emotional powers in my dreams, wild feeling, wild thought. In his writings, he is a friend of wild imaginings. One of his book titles, *Taming Wild Thoughts* (1997), perhaps chosen posthumously by his daughter, Parthenope, did not seem to do justice to the naked, wild aspect of Bion, although he was a great lion tamer as well. It is not clear how domesticated wild dimensions of psyche can become. I doubt Bion wanted or expected to turn them into British gardens, if that were possible. At the same time, we have to live with frightening, uplifting, downcasting, and exceedingly dangerous aspects of our nature, so some modicum of "peace" with the storm is needed. Near the end of his life, he said he himself had not succeeded in securing equanimity in face of psychic turbulence, although he thought it might be an evolutionary goal, something to which pychoanalysis could contribute. Bion felt it unrealistic if you were not frightened of dangers in a session. I was always struck by the emphasis on peace in Jewish prayer and greeting and could not help but feel it was more wish than reality, a reflection of just how unpeaceful we are.

Many creative people court states outside business as usual. I heard Anton Ehrenzweig speak years ago on seeking states of letting go and dipping in by forcing himself to stay up late at night until he got to the point of writing without knowing what he was writing about. At a later time, he would work the material over and see what he could use. He warned artists not to throw out what they have done in a kind of aesthetic hangover the morning after. Sit with it and let it develop. Paradoxically, it appears that some of Marion Milner's greatest moments of peace came in expanded states of awareness through processes of creative immersion. In Ehrenzweig's book, *The Hidden Order of Art* (1993), he delineated phases and moods of creative work (Freud placed great emphasis on mood in creativity). One moment you might feel like a god scanning great vistas from thrilling heights, the next feel that the work is shit. He writes of the importance of endurance, going through the various moods and phases, letting work build. In one passage, he described Picasso sitting for hours staring at a work in progress, not knowing what to do next, emphasising the importance of waiting. One can apply this to the importance of creative waiting in therapy sessions as well. Levinas (1999; Eigen, 2005) writes of the importance of creative waiting at the edge of impasse and evolution. In politics perhaps, more waiting, fewer wars.

Bion remarks that the Death Pit of Ur was in a rubbish dump. He could imagine a priest making prayers as the mass descent into the pit occurred, sanctifying the ground, perhaps music in the background. The rubbish dump becoming holy ground, the descending souls elevated. Yet, intuition links rubbish with dead bodies as well. Here is part of religious power at work, a sense of elevation uniting people, even unto death. What Bion might call counterparts, or a constant conjunction: ascent–descent.

I often wonder what kind of hypnotic spell, or other kinds of spells, bind soldiers in war. It is noble and, at times, necessary for survival to defend your country. I remember a film where one soldier becomes afraid and leaves his troop, deserts out of fear. In his case, I felt a triumph of sanity. His body is more sane than emotional–mental ideology, oughts, shoulds, musts. The call of the body, another kind of must, in this case affirming one's life, a need to save one's life.

How many times in therapy have I heard someone condemn themselves for being a coward when often the so-called "cowardly" course they took was an act of sanity. For example, the psychotic man who stood up to the god command within and could not throw himself in front of a subway train. He could not live with himself for not obeying the command. His failure branded him a coward forever. "What would have happened," he wondered, "if I were brave enough, true enough to follow the Voice?" A bit like Abraham lifting his hand to slay Isaac. Abraham went all the way, my psychotic patient aborted the moment and could not forgive himself.

It is a true blessing of therapy, when it works, to allow for time for one process to subside, another to increase. Without quite knowing what happened, little by little, months and years went by and one day my patient awoke to realise the need to throw himself in front of a train in order to be true no longer had currency. Not that it totally disappeared, but its strength diminished, occupied less psychic space. He no longer believed in it although small doubts lingered. He felt his own life feelings more centre stage, the will of the body, the care of the soul, already far out of the psychotic eggshell. Emotional colour was not lost but went elsewhere, into more satisfactory living. Is this an instance of what religions call saved? O Lord, please save me from You? Or, in this case, saved from a god manqué, a false god within.

What if the retinue accompanything the queen to the Death Pit of Ur woke up to their body? What if their body states woke them up, like the soldier, like my psychotic patient? "My body doesn't want to be here, but I have to do it for my country, for my Queen, for my community, because I have to." What if body states jolted a shift in awareness and one became afraid for one's life and valued one's life over musts, communal constraints? What if one felt and said, "I want to live" and acted on it? Cowardly sanity? Why cowardly at all? Are there not ways in which following mass ideology and commands can be "cowardly"? At times we are at a loss. Madness is built into the body. Sanity is built into the body. So-called neurotic–psychotic indecision can be caught in a swinging door. I have always valued psychotic indecision as a bit of sanity, or residue or refuge of sanity. In its way, akin to Levinas's, Bion's, Ehrenzweig's waiting, akin to mystic not-knowing, a forced way of staying open to possibility without realising it. It might take ten to twenty years for appeciation of inaction in such moments to develop. Quite a turn in therapy, siding with birth and development of creative inaction over cowardly bravery, throwing one's life away by jumping in front of a train.

Scholarship seems at odds. Wooley, the original excavator of Ur, felt the Queen's court and servants went down the pit "voluntarily" and took their places with the Queen's sanctified corpse. Some later scholars said that servants being dressed in finery shows evidence of their having been knocked out. Another later researcher found evidence of a preservative that acted as a poison.

The pit that gets filled. If you know Bion, you know he writes about pits, auditory and optic pits among them. If you know Melanie

Klein, you know she wrote about the stomach pit as a source of agon for the infant, pain of hunger without a frame of reference for the infinity of pain, the pit of hell. Bion felt auditory and optic pits were remainders from prehistoric times, or fish time, residues from pre-human life. Pre-human remainders, he feels, that might have repercussions for what we are like, influencing consciousness, thinking, feeling. Bion showed special interest in the optic pit and the white light it might produce in the womb owing to pressures that come and go. The light that is translated to the Light within, associated with vision and wisdom, backdrop for adventures in criminality and enlightenment, a backdrop of "unstained white radiance", foil, yet stimulus, for dialectic between purity and corruption.

Bion goes mainly by Wooley's account, envisioning a leaf of forgetfulness drip, which Bion associates with hashish, which I suspect must have been stronger. Then the dark, sublime night of visions, followed by night alone. A powerful force at work throughout human life, in individual and group activity, including psychoanalysis. A strong force that Bion insists we know nothing or little about. He puts a barium tracer on it. There are many ideas about it. But a main thrust of his work is to uncover, or, at least, note, it for further experience, meditation, observation. He says repeatedly little is as yet known about this force that so much is written about.

About three hundred years after the burials, thieves plundered the site at Ur. Lots of valuables were buried in the pit. Bion imagines their fear, the taboo against disturbing the dead. Surely they had trepidations, spoiling the rest of spirits. The fear of spirits of the dead was alive in those times, perhaps more than in ours. Dread of avenging spirits plagued the mind and often still does.

What could their state of mind be? Greed and lust for riches in tension with fear? Were they scared to death as they made a hole straight down into the burial pit near where the Queen and her riches lay? Their stalwart precision, determination, and skill struck Bion as a scientific triumph. A victory of curiosity and desire over dread. Plunder they did, although much was left over for Wooley. After a time, the latter got tired of finding golden ornaments, wanting something more revealing. Did the thieves take all they could, all they dared to, enough to satisfy their hunger? Siding with hunger over taboo and dread seemed to Bion a psychological achievement. The thieves were daring and skilful.

Psychoanalysis and anthropological psychology offer many probes into archaic levels of mind, primitive dreads. They offer many reflections, yet are far from exhausting speculative reason. For Bion, these marauders seemed almost heroic, driven by another set of values, not merely mesmerised by religious force or drug, but by jewels and riches, a dynamic we are familiar with today. I want—I want the treasure. Mesmerised, perhaps, by a "new" drug: I want. At once a breath of fresh air, freedom, and excitement before being trapped by one's own momentum (even if hundreds of years later).

Bion felt a statue should be erected in their honour as forerunners of science. They endured dread of spirit to satisfy curiosity and greed, withstanding pressures that would terrify a less scientific spirit. What turns things take over time. One can speak now of scientific greed and financial greed as two of the ruling spirits of the day.

So, that is one story of a state of mind, a crazy monarchical–political–religious state of mind. How many of you would want to die with your queen? Yet, there are probably psychological ways we do just that in one form or another. Think about it in terms of relations with someone close to you, the kinds of things that you get into with these forces at work. Perhaps not exactly caught between greed and plunder and religious mania and obedience, but not too far from variations on related themes. I do not think a single person in this room would want to die with their king or queen, yet think of the ways this plays out in your psychology in daily life. Psychoanalysis, in part, is a meditation on destructive imperatives that paralyse our sense of life. Did we gain a tiny bit of sanity in four thousand years? Maybe a tiny bit. Many die for their country, right or wrong, in deaths much worse than the Great Death Pit of Ur. I am told that in Israel, if you are newly married, you are exempt from the army for a year. A tiny bit of sanity? Is more possible? Sanity creeps in here and there.

Bion conjoins being buried with your queen with the plundered grave, two states of being that might be related, two sets of impulse, one more religious, one more scientific. It is as if what is expressed by religion and what is expressed by science are competing sides of our nature. Tendencies or attitudes or states that go through a variety of relations, interacting–dissociating, co-nourishing–mutually antagonistic: a challenge that eggs us on to new ways of conceiving ourselves.

* * *

Bion evokes another, related, state of mind with the story of Palinurus in the *Aeneid*. After Troy was defeated, the Trojans sailed to Italy. Palinurus was assigned to lead the fleet, so kept his eyes on the stars in order to navigate. Now, you know the Greek and Roman gods and characters in their stories represent many states we have. Can we count the states we have? Just think about it. All the Hindu gods and stories, so many states of being. And then there are less constellated states without number or name, and states yet to be experienced and communicated, akin to de Chardin's (1959; Bion, 1994) noosphere. Maybe we should all talk about God knows what, whatever it is. I once took a Heidegger course with William Richardson, and he invited us to speak with him informally at his apartment. We were talking about experience and communication, how so much is beyond expression. He straddled both worlds and finally said, "What do we do, sit all day and say ugh?" Yet, when I read Rilke, I feel feeling life is coming into being with words. I feel that when I read Bion and Winnicott, too.

Palinurus, steadfast, experienced, doing his job, eyeing the stars, steering the ship, and, as if out of Pandora's box, out of the blue, a Roman god pops up like the devil in Punch and Judy. Somnus, god of sleep, son of "Night", twin of "Death", attempts to lull Palinurus, seducing him to sleep, everyone is sleeping, your eyes are getting tired, someone will take your place. Palinurus resists temptation, says no, I wouldn't be a man if I failed to steer this ship through. That was too much for Somnus who threw Palinurus overboard. Just like that! Palinurus gone, his screams unheard. In an instant—gone!

This story appeals to Bion as a bit of alpha–beta work because it demonstrates a pattern that characterises all of Bion's clinical vignettes. A sudden change from good to bad (Bion, 1994; Eigen, 1999, 2001b, 2011a). On the grid it is Row C, myth, but also Column 3, notation of an experience characterised by sudden change of state, something bad happening, a drop into the abyss, akin to sudden psychic death (Eigen, 1996). Bion studies nuances of catastrophic change. Alpha begins to formulate unknown beta impact in terms of image and story, calling attention (Column 4) to a sudden, unpremeditated blow. Alpha work begins the study (Column 5) of catastrophic impact, formulating it this way by means of dream and mythic narrative and, eventually, conceptual thought (Rows D–F). A sudden hit out of the blue that one is not prepared for and does not have the capacity to work with. All of Bion's clinical vignettes have this structure and his choice of Palinurus and Somnus illustrates it. His work studies, even attempts to digest, or at least note and call attention to, this state of affairs. It is, I feel, a crucial state for humanity to begin and continue to process, building capacity as we go.

Winnicott (1992; Eigen, 2004, 2009, 2011a), in his way, calls attention to personality being hit as personality begins to form. Traumatised beginnings can leave a persistent fear of beginnings in one's life, beginnings as a signal of disaster.

Bion magnifies the catastrophic moment. We have learnt a good deal about this moment, the shock, freezing, hardening yet acute sensitivity, paralysing fear–rage, deadening, being put out of play. I once heard a speaker say, when asked about the difference between a schizophrenic and psychopath, one is all wound, the other scar tissue. True or not, a feel for catastrophic processes comes through.

One way Bion calls attention to this state of affairs is by talking about a twinship of omnipotence–helplessness. Swings, fusions, antagonisms between states: king of the mountain, at the bottom the next. It is hard to underestimate the importance of this twinship. I am God omnipotent and react with godly anger if you cross me (Eigen, 2002), resourceless in the face of forces that smash and smash and smash.

Palinurus, one moment strong, in control, self-assured, the next hurled into the z-dimension. A moment we wrestle and work with all life long.

*   *   *

Minus fifty and beyond minus-z dimensions: I have hinted that I sense many minus levels beyond fifty, many z dimensions. Infinities of minus and plus z dimensions. I suppose I want to feel that no one is beyond help or, in old language, beyond redemption. I want to feel that no one is beyond trying. I might be wrong, but I do not want to believe so. Perhaps, especially, for myself. Yet, things I felt beyond change in my thirties have, at least partly, given way in my seventies. Facing death helps.

Yet, I am told facing death does not help everyone. It is common wisdom that some crumble in the face of the end, die of depression as well as disease. I knew someone who had an inoperable brain tumour that was sure to shorten his life and did. His doctors and family never told him. Palliative cobalt treatments were rationalised as life saving.

I felt it cruel to keep the truth from him, but I no longer am sure what is good or bad for a person at a given time. Deep down, I felt he knew and had made preparations, opened his heart in ways no one can know unless they feel it too.

Surely, the idea that the Hebrew people corrected a set of faults in the days between leaving Egypt and meeting God on Mount Sinai is an idealisation, a giant inspirational fib, one I find depressing. I used to try to correct my faults and thought I could. Who did I not listen to, Norman Vincent Peale, Benjamin Franklin, Dale Carnegie, you name it. New Year's resolutions, Yom Kippur ablutions—to no avail. Little by little, help came from elsewhere, bits of psychoanalysis, bits of wisdom literature, bits of experiencing the opening–closing heart, bits of living, lucky moments, lucky meetings. Hard to pin down dialectics between struggle and Grace. The aching heart, the caring heart. Will-power, control alone, did not do it. The Power had to come from Somewhere Else.

I read in the *Tanya* (Zalman, 1973) that there is such a thing as a perfect *tzaddik* (sage, righteous one), one who has transformed the evil impulse and no longer has to struggle with it. I have never met such a person and doubt one exists. It is an ideal image. Whether you should or should not strive for this is very individual and depends on many factors. What is good for one person at a particular time is disastrous for another. It is an image that can be persecutory, more hindrance than help. It depends. At the same time, if one takes Rabbi Zalman's depiction not as a final ideal to achieve in this life, but as a thread that is part of many moments more or less, it gains currency and value and possibility, part of dialectics between struggle and Grace, part of the braided *challah* of existence (the term "braided dream challah" taken from a Shomer Zwelling posting on my Yahoo! group; see Chapter Two of this work).

In contrast, an image that helped me thaw out a little more was a painting of a failed saint, part of an exhibit by the Japan Society in New York City some years ago. The saint was coming down a mountain, having failed to achieve enlightenment. What care the artist gave this "failure", which helped loosen something clenched in me. When I hear about all that I have to correct that is beyond me, I tighten.This man's failure was releasing. So—someone knew.

Why call the level beyond redemption fifty? Perhaps to help organise a child mind. Fables are important. They help one live. When

I was young, I read novels avidly, which I searched to learn how to live. How to face the vision of infinities of malignancies, goodness, creativity? The great sandwich of existence. Plus and minus grids, plus and minus *Sephirot*, plus and minus z dimensions.

The work of reversal, the work of the negative, doing–undoing. Palinurus—I know what I'm doing, the ego steering the ship—goodbye Palinurus. Freud's depictions of the ego as master of its house enduring humiliation, mortification. The ego, thrown overboard in so many ways, reforms. Bion asks, how do we begin to digest the state that Palinurus represents, a speck in a constellation largely unknown?

Plus and minus grids with ultra–infra processes, including processes off the grid, not only beyond understanding, but beyond ordinary perception, perhaps making themselves known by dimly sensed perturbations. Perhaps partly perceivable, partly not. Infinities of minus grids, minus z dimensions. Not just doing the work of destruction, undoing what is built, but opening pathways not yet known, yet to emerge.

Dr Z in *Flames From the Unconscious* (2009) was conceived as living in Winnicott's z-moment, the moment of permanent alteration for the worse. He lives there because that is his work. His calling is to work in and with the z-dimension, life permanently deformed. Someone has to work there, one cannot just write "malignant regression" off. It is our work. By "our", I mean all of us, if we keep evolving. If we learn, more and more, little by little, to work with what cannot be worked with. My suspicion is that if we do not do this work, life will continue to be subject to our destructive tendencies. The latter are part of life. To make destruction go away, we would have to make life go away. But there is destruction and destruction. Because we cannot do everything (become perfect saints depicted by Zalman and others) does not mean we can do nothing. There are ways we can learn to be partners with ourselves, partners with our capacities, partners with experience. Ways we can, over time, make a positive difference. Bion has warned us that whatever we do, we are in danger of undoing it—a Tower of Babel complex (Eigen, 2011a). Let us take this suspicion to heart and see if paying attention in a caring way can, at least somewhat, modify it. My experience is that the z-dimension is packed with creative power. The energy of the universe has immense destructive power and yet gives birth to creative life.

Sometimes, I play with the letter Z. Zohar, Zalman, zebra, Zorba (which I am told has to do with life, "live each day"). I picture an hourglass with sands of life (as in sand drawings). On the top is fullness, overflow, abundance. On the bottom, nothingness, emptiness, nullity, humility. Two kinds of openness. Sometimes, unexpectedly, bottom and top reverse, sometimes fuse. Or appear as a double helix, interwoven, interpenetrating, interpermeating "braided dream *challah*".

*   *   *

In the beginning of the *Zohar*, there is a phrase: "There is a rose and there is a rose!" The *Zohar* interprets this to mean the children of Israel, God's special rose. I interpret it as different states of being, for example, an everyday, just plain me state, and a state of heightened experiencing. Or, perhaps, "lower" and "higher" states. Or, perhaps, states of struggle and Grace.

Now, I like just plain everyday me. At this point, heading towards eighty, I wish I could go on being just plain me for a very long time. *Dayenu*—it is quite enough. I would be satisfied. Why does my God-given equipment add all the extras, such as infinity? Or is it that infinity runs through the whole package, even everyday me? Empirical me, psychological me, transcendental me. Everyday living, constant struggle, Grace. Braided together, more than braided, within each other, permeating each other. Hmmm . . . I'll take the Grace state – can we pick and choose?

"There is a rose and there is a rose!" A really optimistic passage— nothing wrong with being a "rose" or a "rose!" Like it or not, we have this double capacity. There is nothing wrong with just being all right, but there is also heightened reality, heightened possibility. Possibly a moment of enlightenment, or being taken somewhere by music or Eros, or simply walking down a street. If you have ever suffered enforced confinement, being able to just walk down a street, gently letting your arms swing, is bliss. For me, it is ecsatsy to go out my door, take a few steps, and say, "God, I'm still here. Thank you!"

James (in his introduction) talked about the good feeling he had just getting through the caesura of 6th Avenue, through all the bikes that are out today. It is a beautiful sunny day and I am hoping to run around Prospect Park three times after this meeting. Just me running around the park. But what happens when you run, all the states you go through, tired legs crawling, not being able to go another step, slowing down, taking it easy, then after a while flying. You cannot stop it.

When I was young, I tried to stop it as an experiment. I must have been around twenty-one or twenty-two, misapplying Descartes's radical doubt. Radical doubt as a psycho-spiritual exercise, doubting everything, rip everything apart, let nothing stand. One day, in Twin Peaks, San Francisco, I came across a deserted lot with a tree in the middle. The bareness of the little lot touched me, something empty and bare in me resonating, something naked. The tree in the middle suddenly felt like grace itself, full, cup runneth over. Empty and full at the same time. A heightened sense of poignant beauty grew, ecstatic beauty. Whoa, I said, applying radical doubt, let's kill it. In those days, I totally misconceived what Descartes meant. I did not understand epistemological doubt. For me it was existential doubt, real doubt, total doubt. Could anything survive it?

I tried to knock the tree in the lot experience out and the more I tried to kill it, the more it kept coming back. The experience kept asserting itself and finally I gave in. Beauty won. Wow! Which is a word I am told Steve Jobs said as he was dying. Wow! This orgasmic experiential capacity can overtake you at any time. It can be almost anything any moment. *Can.* So there's a rose and a rose, an experience of abundance, fruitfulness, fecundity—this wondrous experience we have. A rose that lights everything up.

*   *   *

In one Kabbalah–Chassidus story, a sage was told to seek another sage, a happening common in Buddhist stories, too. A vision or enlightenment quest in the spirit of the Tao. The journeyer comes to the sage's house in the middle of the night when the latter was with students. The seeker joined the *Torah* study. Arguments about interpretations grew and the atmosphere became more contentious. *Torah* fights are not unusual, like Zen "fights" or contests, each vying for a particular view or experience of reality. Spiritual fights. Disagreements in the *Talmud* are a matter of course. Some feel opposition makes you stronger. Rabbi Nachman tells us that there are phases where opposition makes you weaker. Too much premature opposition can kill faith before it is born. But, at a certain point, opposition can strengthen faith, sharpen it.

At last the late night study session ends, the students leave, and the two sages are alone together. The newcomer says to the older sage, "I saw a furnace, living coals when you were speaking. I felt you were getting to the bottom of things."

The older sage confesses, "I really don't care for discussions like this. I don't like arguing about things. What does it add to the glory of God, these arguments? Maybe it has uses but it does not go where you need to go, the deepest level. You need to go deeper than the arguing place."

Hearing this, the younger sage decides he will stay with the older one forever. At last, a teacher. So there is study and there is study! (This and some other of the stories here are rewrites of commentaries found in *Living Waters*, Leiner, 2001.)

Another story: a wedding. A father is making arrangements for his son's wedding and feels nothing is good enough. The food isn't quite right, this, that not good enough. He keeps picking fault, drives his servants crazy. Everyone is doing their best. At some point, he suddenly has a vision. He pictures his son's joy on his wedding night, his son's joy throughout the day. In face of this joy, the father's pickiness goes away. He got in touch with the thing itself.

A little like the Martha and Mary story. Martha welcomes Jesus into her home and tends to chores to make his stay more comfortable, while her sister Mary stays with him, listening to wisdom words. The state symbolised by Martha is useful everyday care, but distracts her from the food of the Lord that Mary enjoys. Two attitudes, both needed. Do not live by bread alone but every word that comes from the mouth of the living God. Indeed, one blesses the bread and sanctifies it. But the bread that comes from the heart of a sage—there is bread and there is bread!

* * *

One meaning of *matzah* is strife. There was a rabbi who said, "A scholar in strife, torn apart in his heart, that's the one I want to stay close to." This was in back of my mind when I saw a man who had been coming to me for about two years, a very depressed man. He was noticeably better, but still very depressed. Even though he was improving, he was always threatening to leave because his depression did not go away. I think he needs a different psychopharmacologist, but so far he has not followed my suggestion. Often, he begins by threatening to leave but, by the session's end, enough has happened so that he comes again. Something like Scheherazade.

The rabbi I just spoke of, the one who feels close to those torn by strife, also said, "How do I know a student is for me? If he doesn't talk about going home." A lot of students, after leaving home, become homesick and keep talking about going home. Such a one is not for this rabbi. A student who does not talk about going home—that one has made an attachment to the teacher, his new home, his appetite, his desire whet for the new. In such a case, spiritual need and hunger trump homesickness.

So, my depressed patient. He was getting up to leave at the end of a session and we were in limbo. Will we see each other next week? Nothing happened this time to whet his appetite for more. As he is getting up he speaks about his emotional pain some more, and I said, "Does it scare you that your distress brings me closer to you?" The rabbi I just told you about was in my mind; I almost heard him speaking as I spoke. My patient started crying instantaneously and I started crying. We were in tears because his distress brought us close. We continued cliff hanging. I rarely try to make people stay, unless I fear something destructive. I do not feel indispensable. There are so many good workers in this field, so many possible avenues for help. It is good to feel you can leave if you have to, people who need a safety hatch. What stops them from leaving in such a situation is not a must but Scheherazade's story, the possibility of a further state, another happening, another moving moment, the potato chips of therapy.

* * *

Everyone knows the psalms, but look at what is in them.

Listen to my supplications. Answer me in your faithfulness.

Do not enter into strict judgement with your servant for no living creature will be innocent before you, for the enemy pursued my soul.

He ground my life into the dirt.

He sat me in utter darkness like those who are long dead.

When my spirit drew faint upon me, within me, my heart was appalled.

I recalled days of awe. I pondered over all Your deeds, I spoke about Your handiwork, I spread out my hands to You, my soul longs for You like the thirsty lamb.

Answer me soon!

Oh, Hashem, my spirit is spent. Conceal not your face from me. Must I be like those who descend into the pit?

Let me hear Your kindness at dawn, for in You I have placed my trust.

Let me know the way I should walk, for to You have I lifted my soul.

Rescue me from my enemies, Hashem. I have hidden my plight from all but You.

Teach me to do Your will for You are my God. May Your good spirit guide me over level ground.

Revive me. Remove my soul from distress and with Your kindness cut off my enemies and destroy all who oppress my soul for I am Your servant.

*   *   *

Read the psalms. Find lines, passages that speak to you. More than speak to you—speak through you from the deepest parts of existence, letters to you from the depths.

Put aside what puts you off. There is much in the psalms that is parochial, narrow pleas for help with enemies, pleas to destroy enemies. We are told these songs were written by warrior musicians. You might not want to be part of war, vengeance. Do not let them ruin psalm jewels for you, a voice deeper than your heart. Yet, do not entirely castigate and feel above negative sentiments, fear, anger and self-serving. You will find them in you.

We all have enemies that pursue our soul, enemies within our soul, within our own house, persecutory elements that blight existence. No one can destroy all the enemies in one's soul, even if that were desirable. That will not happen. Enemies within are part of who we are, part of inner drama. We interact with our enemies all life long. Do we learn anything? Do we deepen? What would life be like without them? "How long, how long, O Lord?" the psalmist cries. How long will they keep me from You? Why do You bring me close to You this way, the deepest pain a bridge and barrier.

The psalmists knew about utter darkness. How long ago was this, three thousand years? Over and over, psalms trace a drama of being closer to–further from the beloved, wellsprings from the Source, the One. Over and over, they trace dramas of utter darkness, living death, and revival. Two great, intertwining soul dramas that mark existence, basic rhythms, rhythms of faith. The faith that constitutes us, that sears our depths, appeals to and springs from God's faithfulness. It is only in the latter that Life is possible. There is life and there is Life!

From the psalms we learn a lot about our makeup, who we are. It almost seems we are helpless in face of ourselves. What can we do with ourselves, our attacking, vain nature, our desolation and need for closeness with the One, valleys of death and kindness, the great You we live in, closer than ourselves. "I am Your servant," the psalmist says, a confession, a wish, a plea from the heart.

What can be done in face of ourselves? Not what we would like, perhaps, but more than we think, miracles of every day. More than tastes of Grace. Living in the Grace dimension as a thread of existence. You are fooling yourself if you think your enemies will vanish in your lifetime. They are part of you, but your relationship with each other can change. Your relationship with yourself can change. It might be that you cannot get rid of the fatal flaw without getting rid of yourself. But you cannot rid yourself of Grace either, the work it does, the places it takes you. Doors open when the "flaw" meets Grace. At night, you put your head upon the pillow and go into God. There is none else, a place to live from when you wake.

(Applause.)

*   *   *

Any thoughts or questions? We have a few moments.

Question: I love the Psalms of David. I feel such an affinity with him but am horrified. I found myself wondering if he wrote these line after his son died. What happened when his son became his enemy? One of the most poignant lines of the Bible haunts me. "Would God I had died for thee O Absolom, my son, my son."

Response: The Bible has many voices, many moments, one of the deepest, heartbreak, the heart torn apart that the sage wants to be close to. Our need not to turn our broken heart away. If you can get past trying to literalise the Bible or be a "fundamentalist", but find the letters inscribed in your heart, as you have, you find it goes for the jugular, hits the jugular, heart, and guts over and over. It's all there, right? The pain in the Bible, the personal cry, there's scarcely anything like it, except in our own private selves.

*   *   *

On another note, let me share a little vignette from Chuang Tzu, one of my favourites. I am adapting, partly rewriting, partly quoting, a story from Burton Watson's edition of *Chuang Tzu: Basic Writings* (1964, pp. 80–82). I call this story, "The Crookedy Man".

Sudden illness hits Master Yu and Master Ssu visits him. "How are you?" he asks, deeply concerned. "Amazing!" said Master Yu. "The Creator is making me all crookedy like this! My back sticks up like a hunchback and my vital organs are on top of me. My chin is hidden in my navel, my shoulders are up above my head, and my pigtail points at the sky. It must be some dislocation of the yin and yang! . . . My, my! So the Creator is making me all crookedy like this!"

The passage goes on to detail Master Yu's lack of resentment and possible things the Creator might turn him into in lives to come, like turning his arm into a crossbow to shoot game for food, "or perhaps in time he'll transform my buttocks into cartwheels . . . my spirit for a horse and I'll go riding". Master Yu very much seems to accept the turns of life and death, the Creator's transformations. Whenever I read this story, I smile inside, feel wonder, appreciation and sometimes peace. How unfathombly moving, to be part of life's creative activity. I wonder if Death and Destruction Itself feels this awe.

The passage goes on to tell of another man, Master Lai, becoming ill, about to die, and he, too, tells his mourners to respect the moment. "Shoo! Get back! Don't disturb the process of change! . . . How marvelous the Creator is! What is he going to make out of you next? Where is he going to send you? Will he make you into a rat's liver? Will he make you into a bug's arm?"

Master Lai speaks of going into death with the trust of a child listening to his parents. ". . . If I think well of my life, for the same reason I must think well of my death . . . I think of heaven and earth as a great furnace, and the Creator a skilled smith. Where could he send me that would not be all right?"

Now, my guess is that many here could easily think of lots of life forms and places which are not all right! More than not all right— absolutely horrifying! Master Lai wondered what sort of inauspicious material he would be if he refused the Creator's transformations. This, of course, is no answer to the critique of being we all feel. Surely, some of us suspect we could have done better, if we were the Great Smith. Or, at least, the Great Smith *should* have done better. No one solves questions like these.

Did you notice that, in different ways, Masters Yu and Lai and Job come to the same place? Entering the hour glass at different points, yet coming to the same Point of Marvel (Eigen, 2011b, 2012a, 2014). This will not still your doubt and critique and attempts to make things better. We are partners in this. But don't do yourself the disservice of missing what they found. Listen within and hear.

*   *   *

Question: I want to thank you. I want to risk putting into words what should probably be expressed only as an exhalation of breath. I do experience this as a coming into contact with the boundless background support that you speak of. I do. There's a place I'm most alone and it's in writing I venture off the edge of the earth and experience revelation. And then think, this is shit. And that's where I most struggle. It's there that what I experience here says to me keep going, you're going in the right way, in that place where I'm most alone but where everything of spiritual importance happens to me. Thank you.

Response: Thank you, too. We should all keep going. For those who may not know it, in *Flames from the Unconscious: Trauma, Madness, and Faith* (2009), the first two chapters, I write about Winnicot's sense of aloneness and how the baby's sense of aloneness can become traumatised, wounded aloneness. Even aloneness needs support. A baby might be unaware of the support its aloneness receives. Much of the support the mother gives the baby is not cognised, perhaps wrapped in an implicit sense of unknown boundless support. In part, this inherent sense of boundless, unknown support in the background of our beings, allows aloneness to develop into an aloneness that is worthwhile. You seem to tap into it through writing. Writing allows you to go through many states in the faith journey, the shit and the goodness.

Question: I think it was Rilke who wrote that we madly gather the honey of the visible to store in the great golden hive of the invisible. But I was thinking we madly gather the honey of the invisible also. So much invisible today. And you just opened up the psalms for me. I thought, well, that's what we need, a course on the honey of the psalms and store it in the great golden hive of the invisible. Thank you.

Response: I love that. The hives of the invisible. So much of our insides, known and unknown, in the psalms. Sometimes, I feel that in addition to the visible writing we see on the page or the music we hear inside us, the psalms also have invisible writing, unhearable music, and some of it gradually makes itself known, like invisible ink becoming seeable by dipping visible words in our souls. I sometimes imagine a course, reading the psalms from a deeply psychological view, touching invisible depths.

Question: Mike, thank you. I think people are saying they hope the process at work here today continues in some way. In terms of the aloneness you just mentioned, could you say a couple of words about "wounded aloneness" in your other work, particularly with addictions?

Response: This is the fifth seminar I have given in the past few years for the NYU Contemplative Studies Project, and I expect to take a break for a while, but I do give an open seminar every Tuesday and have an online Yahoo! group.

The first two NYU Kabbalah and psychoanalysis seminars were expanded and published as *Kabbalah and Psychoanalysis* by Karnac; the second two, also expanded and published by Karnac is titled *A Felt Sense: More Explorations in Psychoanalysis and Kabbalah*.

It sounds as if you read or anticipated my chapter, "Spirituality and addiction", in *Flames From the Unconscious*, something I have given much thought to, since addiction of some kind, including addiction to aspects of personality, is part of many lives. I suspect at least part of the dynamics of substance addiction involves an attempt to create a state of unwounded aloneness, to undo wounded aloneness. It won't work because you cannot successfully undo a wound just by wishing it away. I am not against taking drugs or courting alternative states, for example, psychedelic experiences and revelations. They can change your life for the better if they don't harm you, kill you, or drive you mad, or diminish motivation or organisational capacity to meet life. It might even be that plant-based chemicals played a role in the origin of religious and visionary experience, homo spiritus. Whatever soma is, I would have liked to try it.

It is important to have your aloneness supported so that it can develop. Aloneness has a biography as part of your personality and needs nourishment and growth opportunities. Some care-givers have a hard time tolerating an infant's aloneness and, on the other hand, some drop the infant into an abyss of aloneness more like an isolation chamber. Here is an example of the former in *The Psychotic Core*, which some of you know. When I was in my early twenties, working with schizophrenic children, a young girl climbed into a baby carriage and lay there for some time, growing more and more relaxed. She lay with her arms up parallel to her head, body open, undefended. A moment of peace, very rare.

Her therapist, a good, active worker, saw the girl lying in the carriage and went over to her and playfully poked her finger in the girl's chest a few times saying, "Poop!" The girl looked alarmed, her body tightened, peace shattered. Shock waves went through me. It seemed to me the little girl's alone state was disregarded not out of malevolence but benevolent playfulness. I think of a video Beatrice Beebe made of a mother needing to keep her baby stimulated, not letting it look away and gather itself together. The mother kept entertaining the baby, going after her look and smile, as the baby tried to turn away. For some infants, in some moments, this might be fun and lead to a burst of pleasure. But there also are moments when this disrupts the baby's rhythm, when the baby is calling for time out.

Towards the end of his transitional obect paper, Winnicott (1953) describes a case in which the mother could not let her child's affect ebb, as if the child had to always be emotionally on to keep the mother in life. The child was robbed of a chance to just be, let her affect spontaneously drop away and enjoy nothingness for a time. It can be quite a burden to have to be "on" all the time, serving another's need.

The little girl I was watching did not seem to drop out of life, but into it when she climbed into the carriage and relaxed. I wondered if she was creating for herself the kind of peace she hoped to get as a baby with her mother. Her alone being seemed full, face and body a gentle colour tone. I was so shocked that this alone state should be so diregarded. It was like a meteor from out of nowhere, traumatising a blissful moment. Of course, I overdo things. Maybe this is one reason I tend to get along with people in what used to be called malignant states, in the z dimension, because I can go there very quickly. I can outdo most of my patients in imaginative elaborations of states of pain. To most people, what happened might seem innocuous, a little playfulness. A moment of being open, holding on to nothing, just being, then taking a sudden jolt, is a moment that stayed with me to this day. What would it be like living every day with someone who misperceives your states or responds wrongly to them?

I remember watching one of our sons after birth staring into an infinite horizon. When I was with him I began to feel something of this state myself, looking into infinity. Winnicott spoke of shared aloneness as well as aloneness supported by an unknown boundless other (Eigen, 2009, 2011a). Imagine what it would be like if your infinity was not supported, growing hunched around traumatic impacts. You can reach these wounded moments in aspects of bodywork, or yoga, or meditation. And even if you cannot fully heal them, a lot opens that might not have otherwise. You go to places you might not have reached without another's support.

Question: I hope this isn't trivialising what we've been talking about, but this is reminding me of a poster that was on the wall of my first astrology teacher's apartment. It was a big poster of the sun saying, "In the beginning was the word and the word was yes." Far below the sun were little people asking, "What did he say?" "I don't know," said someone. And, finally, another person far below said, "He said the word was no! The word was no!" I think our work is about helping people to deal with this misinterpretation.

Response: In the *sephira*, *Malchut*, where we are, there's always yes and no. There's never one without the other for long. So always be ready to change states, rather than force yourself to stay in one state over another.

CHAPTER TWO

On the birth of experience

T he mystery of dreams is deeply connected with the birth of experience. We have an urge to know what dreams mean but often take for granted the field of perception that make dreams possible. Could dreams exist without the seamless perceptual world that seems effortlessly given to us? Dreams make use of the objects of daily life, sky, earth, water, mountains, people, dramas, and, above all, emotions that populate our objects, fear, dread, desire, care, reaching for fulfilment, loss. I say reaching for fulfilment for, I suspect, more dreams abort fulfilment than achieve it. Dreams often express fragmentary states, aborted states, states that break off before a successful end. As if dreams attempt to communicate something unsatisfactory about our fragmentary lives.

One can also posit the opposite, that the perception of our world we take for granted depends on unconscious dream-work. Freud writes that experience of the external world is made possible by projection of internal space. If what he calls "the it" (*das Es*) is the primary psychical reality and ego and superego develop from it, these structures require "space". This view posits the first space as internal psychical space out of contact with external reality that plays a role in structuring growing experience of externality. If the "it" helps to pressure early dreaming processes into existence, partly as a medium dedicated to representing "it-reality", we might say "it" dreams reality into existence as it seeks (creates) more space to extend and exercise itself.

Bion, also, links early experience of space with a sense of affects coming and going, for example, now feeling more filled or empty of affect. This can be tied with the emptiness and fullness associated with hunger and feeding, but not limited to it. The psalms have many examples of feeling empty and full, a sophisticated expression of now more affect, now less, although in the psalms empty and full are tied with the presence–absence of the inner subject-object, God. However, we get a dramatic sense of filled–empty space of the soul with the coming and going of feeling. With Freud, Bion suggests that the space of feeling structures development of our sense of outside space.

On the face of it, it seems absurd to assert that the existence of outside space depends on, and derives from, a sense of affect space, outer space depending on inner space. So many of our images for inner space are drawn from the outside world. One would do better to grant autonomy to our perceptual apparatus and innate processes that develop perception. One needs the frame of external reality for existence to develop. And yet, I am hesitant to dismiss Freud's or Bion's vision, which gives a certain primacy to affective reality. Life experience and clinical work teach me that our affective universe is crucial for the way outside "facts" are coloured. One could be inclusive and say that inner–outer realities co-constitute, interpermeate each other. So often, dominance is given to the outside, when, in covert ways, the former is dominated by elusive inner events. Our perceptual world is an affective perceptual world. Our body is a feeling body.

In spite of everything we know of the interactive nature of reality, I do feel there is an autistic sector in human life. The image of being out of contact with the outside world excites literary and cinematic imagination, for good reason. Balint (1992) writes of an area of creativity as a one-body relation, a going into oneself, a contact with depths deeper than mutuality. He also writes of a harmonious inter-penetrating mix-up of self–other in early life. Going deeper than self–other and being part of self–other go together.

Winnicott (1992) writes of an "incommunicado core", a special, sacred core of self that ought not to be violated by life. At the same time, he writes of the interweaving of mother–infant, although he suspects that often the infant does not know that there is this inter-weaving. We, as outsiders, posit it and imagine we see it. But the self–other mix-up for the infant might lack a sense of the other's contribution to the feel of life. The other contributes a lot without the infant knowing it. For Winnicott, even the infant's sense of aloneness needs support it does not know is there (Eigen, 2009; Winnicott, 1988), an aloneness that is a permanent part of life.

Alone is not the same as autistic but, in certain instances, it is not far removed from it either. Autistic has a pejorative sound because it denotes illness. But I feel it is part of human life for good and ill, and often part of creativity. Mahler and co-authors (2000) see it as an early stage of infancy. I suspect the infant goes through many states, and I hesitate to assign primacy of one over the other. Psychoanalysis has long had a propensity to make one set of experiences primary and others secondary, when they might interweave from near the outset. Perhaps, so to speak, there are co-primary states, co- or multi-primary experiential flows. We are multi-dimensional beings, perhaps from the outset, and various dimensions of experience that we inhabit and that inhabit us have their own histories and developmental arcs.

Both–and is more the rule than either/or. For example, alone–not alone are both part of our experiential lives. Why make one more primary than the other if they co-constitute the fabric of living. Aloneness and together each have their biographies, stories to tell, as do ways they interact with and organise each other.

We have insatiable curiosity about dreams. What do they mean? Are they portents about life? There are many dream systems to draw from and comments about symbols throughout the ages. Ancient texts give examples of those who possess greater dream intuition than others, able foretell future events from dream dramas. Even today, there are those who use dreams as hints about what life direction or course of action to take, which talent, potential, or aspect of self to develop. The mystery of dreams takes us deep into the mystery of life; the mystery of life takes us deep into the mystery of dreams.

We tell each other dreams and ask, "What does my dream mean?" Sometimes, I tell someone and they like what I say; sometimes, I tell someone and they do not like what I say. Sometimes, I say one thing and am already thinking of other possibilities. Bion suggests the request that an analyst reveal the meaning of a dream is not as reasonable as it seems and neither asker nor asked ought give in to the pull for quick understanding. There is a danger of skipping steps and missing processes one needs to go through in order to get closer to the dreaming experience itself. How to get the most out of our dreams involves ongoing learning.

Curiosity and the desire for knowledge open journeys that simple answers fail to meet. I might say something about a dream and, a few minutes later, the patient begins talking about more things. The flow goes back and forth, deepens, contact with feelings takes more turns. Rather than have an answer to the dream, the latter becomes a portal for inner journeys. It is these therapy journeys more than "answers" that enrich living.

Bion (1994, pp. 232–235) goes on to suggest the problem is not the dream, but the emotional experience the dream inhabits, compresses, reveals, obscures, narrativises. The core of a dream is an emotional experience and the obscurity and difficulties inherent in dream meaning are those of emotional life itself.

> And about this emotional experience the patient feels as much as an infant about bumping its head on the floor—it wants to know what it means. An emotional experience, then, is in some respects like a physical experience in that it can be felt to have a meaning; that is to say, it is felt to be an experience from which something can be learnt. (Bion, 1994, p. 232)

In some way, are we always infants when it comes to emotional experience? From many lives I have chanced to be part of and many more heard about but never met, I would have to say that yes, we are infants when it comes to emotional experience. We are told to put our feelings into words and that may have value, but it is a funny phrase, too. Which feelings, what words? Sometimes, I imagine words being lowered like a bucket into wells of feeling, coming up with a bucketful while the wellspring continues on its way. I suspect a control/mastery ideology still usurps appreciation of our condition. How to develop capacities that work well, mediate, and enter into creative relations with our emotional life seems very much an issue. One of the great values of Bion's work is persistent acknowledgement of difficulties we are up against and the problematic nature of emotional life itself.

Without willing it, destructive moments pop out of us, hurting ourselves and others, from injury to those closest, group feuds and hates, and international wars. Behaviour we work with and try to control and swear we will never do again, mount and overcome us time and again. Do we really know who we are, our makeup, how to relate to it in better ways and what these ways might look like? Bion keeps the doors and windows open, his work an incessant exploration of problems many feel on top of but which often prove unsolvable.

Meditation, or speaking about, or living one's way into a dream can bring "coherence to facts previously known but not previously seen to be connected" (Bion, 1994, p. 234). This is a characteristic Bion feels is shared by hypotheses in general, including words as hypotheses, which bring things together in ways not quite seen before. We might say that dreams act as hypotheses or stimulate creative hypotheses that touch on our living reality. Our ideas and feelings about dreams share the same limitations as all mediated productions. They are particular slants at particular moments, relative generalisations, perspectives on realities that could also mean something else. You might say the dream is a shadow cast by emotional reality and our interpretations shadows cast by the dream.

Another example of our quest to express and learn something from and about the emotional reality we live and lives us involves the swing back and forth between paranoid–schizoid and depressive positions (Klein, 1946). Again, Bion relates these to hypotheses about emotional processes, attempts to get close to and learn about lived reality. One way to characterise their interplay is in terms of swings between fragmented states of not knowing and the generation of "a-ha" moments that seem more whole and knowledgeable (insights, gestalts, relatedness of elements). Bion wonders if the coming together of diverse elements in the swing from the paranoid–schizoid to the depressive position means

> anything more than that—the human mind being what it is—the individual from time to time has the experience of observing the harmonious inter-relatedness of these elements, whereas in fact there is no reason to suppose that any such relatedness exists? Elements and relatedness alike are aberrations of the observing instrument. (1994, p. 234)

Where does this leave us? With nothing to hold on to?

Bion develops this line of thinking by contrasting two kinds of emotional experience: (1) one "that is secondary to the attempt to solve a problem"; and (2)

> the experience that consists in trying to solve a problem in which the emotional experience is itself the problem. In the first, it is possible to regard the problem as one of unrelated objects requiring synthesis; in the second, there is probably no way of regarding the problem "as" anything at all. (pp. 234–235)

Note at all times Bion's reference to *experience*, whether referring to experience of observing, analysing, putting together, taking apart, disharmony–harmony, work one does with emotional life, or the experience of running up against a wall, as if meeting emotional life itself, one's analytic tools dropping away in helpless insufficiency. "Psycho-analysis itself is just a stripe on the coat of the tiger. Ultimately it may meet the Tiger—The Thing Itself—O" (1991, p. 112). O here signals unknown emotional reality.

Emotional life itself is the problem with "probably no way of regarding the problem 'as' anything at all". A situation one naturally tries to extricate oneself from by creating what unities one can, giving to airy nothing a local habitation and a name, although one might not necessarily call the unknown airy. In some instances, it might feel dense, compressed, resistant, a fortress of beta walls, at others so dispersed and diffuse that no net could hold it. But these are just ways of speaking of attempts to give meaning to what eludes our meaning making apparatus.

A situation in which emotional life itself is the problem with no way of regarding the problem as anything at all with the equipment we have available. A situation that Bion suggests might be more common than appreciated, whether lasting a longer or shorter time, "a problem that makes demands on the individual's equipment and personality" (1994, p. 235).

Elsewhere (2011a), I noted how the pressure of emotion as unsolvable can lead not to the solution of the problem, but to changes in a person owing to extreme, frustrating exertion. Such a state might lead to madness, suicide, giving up, making what adaptations one can, making the best of a bad job, making creative use of what scraps from the depths one plunders, engages, partners. The barrier, the gap, the abyss, the wall remains, but many wonderful human accomplishments result from the attempt to cross the impasse.

Buddha sitting with the wall of suffering, the pressure of all out, persistent, patient exertion opening personality to nirvana, another mode of being. Bodhidharma sitting facing a wall for nine years, the wall of personality, of being, until personality shifts its Archimedean point.

Reading Bion, I feel, is therapy for the human race, teaching humility in face of emotional reality, which he posits as a core of personality. If we cannot learn to work with emotional being, we remain not only hampered, but in jeopardy (Eigen, 2006). And if emotional reality is inherently unknown and unknowable, at least acknowledging this situation a little, or a little more, provides some medicine against hubris and a nearly ubiquitous sense of being right, the other wrong, a wall of lies, beneficent or malignant, that offers some buffer, some raft in waves of existence.

* * *

While it is true that Bion's therapy for humanity leaves us nothing to hold on to (which itself might be therapeutic), he also suggests tools to use, supporting both sides of our pride–humility twinship. One tool he favours is use of myths. Not the attempt to reduce myths to psychoanalytic understanding, but use of myths to expand the reach of psychoanalytic possibility. He gives as an example Freud's use of the Oedipus story as a way in to psychic reality. "The result was the discovery, not of the Oedipus complex, but of psycho-analysis. (Or is it man, or man's psyche, that is discovered . . .)" (1994, p. 228).

He feels that a good deal of emotional reality finds its way into myths, so that the latter can be used to explore the former. A good circle develops. Working with myths can stimulate the capacity to work with emotional currents, increasing growth of alpha function and intuition and keeping them in good repair. Myths as a kind of psychic gymnasium, not just to exercise capacity, but to bring the latter into being and stimulate functioning.

We are probably hungry, even starving for, contact and work with emotional reality, even though so much entertainment contains prisms and shards, mixtures of nourishment and toxins. Too much of the latter act as quick hits, whiffs of processes that need patient living with, attending, investigating, although some offer deep contact and food for thought. Bion suggests picking myths that have stood the test of time as being likely to have more telling psychic content than ephemera and vogues, useful as the latter sometimes are.

He (Bion, 1994, pp. 237–241; Eigen, 2011a) advocates that the analyst select myths relevant to his own life and free-associate to them, to each of the elements in a myth as well as a sense of the whole. He is less interested in using myths in sessions, certainly not in any abstract or imposing way, than in the analyst thawing out his own psychic functioning, for example, opening more capacity to use processes depicted by the first three rows of the grid (Figure 2, p. 26). Humility, because the work is so individual, unique, buckets of infinities; pride because creative exercise of capacity, frustrating as it might be, opens and shapes possibility.

The therapy situation provides a special, limited milieu for birthing or exercising contact with feelings and patterns of feelings in a more sustained, concentrated way than usual. It supports exploration of a psychosphere, cousin of the noosphere (de Chardin, 1959; Bion, 1994), finely nuanced psycho-spiritual domains. Here, without apology, one can pay attention to elusive processes one might not be able to access without dedicated support.

One of the side benefits of becoming a therapist is—if one has the need, bent, sensibility—the chance to open psychic reality by systematic exercise of capacities often downplayed by the dominant culture and common sense—dimensions of uncommon sensing crucial for the feel and taste of life. A life that includes working with problematic, invisible emotional currents that add to the richness of being. I once heard Hanna Arendt (Eigen, 2001a) speak of the secret ecstasy of thinking. I feel, too, deep satisfaction and joy in the profound beauty of analysis, while all too cognisant of its pitfalls. The beauty, awe, and wonder of working with the forever unknown.

*   *   *

Bion's (1994; Eigen, 1999, 2001b, 2011a) clinical vignettes tend to emphasise a movement going from good to bad moments. Good feeling followed by bad. One is having a good meal when suddenly someone throws a mug of beer in one's face, or the waitress brings half a cup of coffee, a lapse that spoils everything. One dreams of signalling the train engineer of impending collision but one's attempt to help leads to loss of the signalling arm.

The above are examples Bion gives, but one could draw many from everyday life almost at random. Remarks your partner makes that cut to the bone, where a moment ago you felt the day was good and things were going well. Something injurious, dangerous happening to a child you love, perhaps something you did that was wounding. Freud spoke of a bad word or look stabbing your heart or hitting like a blow to the face. Such stabs or blows are commonplace. For the moment one goes under, like a submarine rocked by a depth charge, and one struggles to regroup. Often, one must wait minutes, hours, days, some people weeks, for a resetting of the self to occur, some people take years, with no end in sight.

The myths Bion chooses to illuminate this psychic pattern involve good or neutral states turning bad. Loss of the Garden of Eden by the advent of further psychic development. The co-operative attempt to build a tower to reach heaven, smashed by a destructive counter-force. Narcissus punished for enjoying his reflection. Punishments that seem harsh for such "crimes". Picture a baby or child enjoying good moments (Eden) or enjoying building capacities (building with blocks or the innate mystery of body or self growing bigger), or relishing the puzzle and pleasure of one's own changing, yet semi-stable image. And pow! Bad moments come, obliterating the good for a time, perhaps accompanied by a sense of shatter and collapse. Good world turned bad.

Here is a primal phase in birth and development of feeling: the wounding of the good. Bion explores in complex ways a moment of shatter that often becomes encrusted with protective gestures enabling survival and development. A situation in which aliveness is lost or diminished in order to protect survival of aliveness. He might call the coupling of the good with bad a constant conjunction, a pairing of emotional elements that go together, an emotive invariant.

The Bible speaks of thawing a heart of stone to a heart of flesh. It is hard to establish timing. Did a heart of flesh turn to stone because of wounding processes? Is the stone merely outer covering? Did what remained of flesh within become hypersensitive, so that impingements are magnified and one is lost in reactive fear–rage, hiding, impulsive striking out? Or is it possible that we are hard to begin with, soft and hard, double capacity, depending on situation and need.

In addition to Eden, Babel, and Narcissus, Bion also mentions Oedipus as a myth to explore known–unknown emotional reality, which, again, drops one into agony. Life is not what it seems, but what it is remains unclear. Suffering is part of it, that seems certain, and, over time, in the unfolding trilogy, Oedipus achieves his version of coming through the worst, perhaps echoing the baby's double directionality, going from good to bad and settling for good enough once more, as the cycle continues.

The good Oedipus may have felt in a position of power crumbling as he discovered lies he did not know he was living. A feeling of goodness based on lies. Does one ever get to solid ground? Complexity piles on complexity. He kills his father without knowing it, a father who wanted to kill him in infancy. Layers of trauma and deception unravel, deceived by life, as life unfolds truths of his existence.

The blind Oedipus was played by blind gospel singers at the Brooklyn Academy of Music many years ago. In this portrayal, he developed a new kind of sight in his last years, as domains of spiritual experience opened. Hints of a new kind of man who might have been buried in the shell of the old.

There are ways pre-truth Oedipus resembled aspects of the biblical Lot, as portrayed by some rabbis (Leiner, 2001). The dimension of consciousness I have in mind is a kind of naïve enjoyment of success. Lot is contrasted with Abraham, who balanced joy with dread. Lot rejoiced in his good fortune without deep thought as to its ultimate Source. Abraham was afraid he might betray the faith that uplifted his life and joined the struggle to maintain it. He knew a wrong step was possible at any time and was mindful of the strong cord that bound him to God. Abraham did not want to be either very wealthy or poor. He valued a portion that enabled him to deepen the link with his Creator, whereas Lot would not be troubled by wealth that came his way and felt less need to keep a balanced perspective. Great as Abraham was, he felt a need to keep his ego in check, servant of God. There is much in this analogy that does not hold, but I use it to contrast two attitudes that are part of our character: naïve enjoyment of the goods at hand and a larger perspective (a contrast similar to the one we talked of earlier between Cain and Abel).

Rabbi Mordechai Yosef of Isbitza wrote, Abraham "desired to know the place where his life essence was intensely joined to the blessed God, and how far it reached" (Leiner, 2001) His life was ever reaching towards increased union with the Divine, and the latter enabled more and more closeness. God-contact, not material riches, was Abraham's core concern, although having enough gave him the freedom to be mindful of this connection without having to worry about poverty. In contrast, Lot simply enjoyed his riches. Abraham and Lot become emblematic of relative spiritual and material attitudes, both parts of our nature with contributions to make.

*   *   *

The contrast Bion makes, good turning into or displaced by bad—a sudden fall from good feeling to shatter, upset, something wrong—is offset by a pattern Winnicott (1992; Eigen, 2004, 2011a) focuses on. Trauma hitting as personality begins to form, with consequent fear of beginnings, followed by spontaneous recovery in sessions and life. In practice, Winnicott emphasises bad turning good, developing resilience, capacity for repair, coming through. One important contribution of therapy is developing a situation in which therapy wounds become part of a sequence in which recovery is possible. The patient (and therapist) get a chance to go through this basic sequence over and over in different ways. The plummet and return. Bion seems to emphasise the plummet and getting stuck in it. Winnicott adds its counterpart, coming through, coming back. Learning to work with the hit so that quality of recovery and return grows, resulting in more capacity to tolerate the build up and shifts of experience. Good feeling to bad, bad feeling to good. A double rhythm of faith and its vicissitudes, repeated in one or another way all life long.

*   *   *

Dreams have long been associated with the birth of experience, as if we dream life into being, dream ourselves into being. As if the world is God's dream. I have heard such images from childhood in many contexts. My mother would sing, "Row, row, row your boat, gently down the stream; / merrily, merrily, merrily, life is but a dream". As I learnt about world religions, over and over, life was associated with dreaming, whether as illusion or unfathomable depths, mystery. Not to mention Freud's emphasis on dreams as a royal road to the unconscious, a kind of psychic archaeology.

I think of one of the scientists in Werner Herzog's film, *Cave of Forgotten Dreams*, saying our species should be named Homo Spiritus, not Homo Sapiens. Cave paintings as old as thirty-two thousand years, realistic yet also dream-like. A fusion of dream and reality, the two working together. Some wonder if plant psychedelics did not play a role in religious experience. We tend to bifurcate dimensions of experience, separate the dreamer from realist. Yet, we also acknowledge how real, super-real, dream experience can feel. I have heard of dying people who came back for a time, disappointed on returning to this plane of life, having tasted something better at the point of death.

And the super-dream quality of Eros at times, beyond reality, beyond Eros. Lifted to places without names. Beyond the Ineffable. Nothing dissolves. Everything is super-intact. Everything dissolves. Places one never dreamt of. Places one can only dream of. And then it happens. Where is Where?

Sometimes, in meditation, I feel curtains, tissues. Insides are delicate tissues. Curtains you almost see through. You feel them somewhere you cannot know about.

At the same time, I am aware that many capacities contribute. Hard and soft qualities, capacities than span dimensions, particular–abstract, finite–infinite, down to earth–heavenly, sensation–memory–perception–feeling–thinking (Eigen, 1986, 1993, 2001b, 2006, 2011a,b, 2012a, 2013). In Dante's Paradise, heaven never stops opening. And here on earth, there is no end to learning.

Veils and filters are part of it. St Thomas said the beauty we experience here is a foretaste of the more whole beatific experience to come, St Paul—through a glass darkly. Plato—shadows on a cave wall. A sense of the More just beyond. Our capacities tease us into thirst for something more complete. Although there are moments, too, when infinity is in a grain of sand or the moon is in all dewdrops. And, sometimes, for moments, we seem to step out of ourselves into the More itself. Again, a taste, a feel, a sense. A need to shed our skins at the same time that skin births sensory worlds. Enter any capacity or set of capacities, something happens. This is part of the meaning of the *sephirot*, the Kabbalah Tree of Life (see Figure 1, p. 3). Enter anywhere, worlds to explore. So, if I focus on dreams for a time, I do not mean to slight any other of our needed capacities, all of which contribute. All have ways of birthing experience.

* * *

Here is a kind of dream dialogue, taken from my Yahoo! online workshop, August 2013. Dreams are viewed many ways. Many are devastating. Some are "blah". Many are uplifting. At the moment, I am picking posts that explore aspects of creative experience and something elusive. In the next few sections, I hope to let some of the dream dialogue from the workshop evolve, veils in the breeze.

Roni-Sue Allen, a nursery school teacher and student of psychoanalysis in Chile: It may not make any practical difference but I've been thinking about dream-work according to Freud, and, you know, the more I think about it, the more I question its creativity and wonder about purposefulness. The world just turned upside down for a moment and the dream-work seems more and more to me like a specific kind of broken record. It doesn't seem so to our waking minds, as we are surprised and delighted to awaken to discover this seeming work of art which has been made in our absence. Something mysterious, because we are not aware of our hand in its construction. Maybe we overvalue mysterious things. I know I do.

Barrie Karp, NYC artist and independent scholar: Accepting the caveat of over-valuation, still, it is real wonderful, wonder-ful creative experience. I was thinking and writing yesterday about how translating dreams, speech especially, forces one to oneness where the dream was not oneness. It feels as if I dream many dreams simultaneously, not sequentially very often, and it feels as if these are among the most poignant dreams, but one never knows if one is digging them deeply enough, and it seems the answer to your question: "dreams *vs.* dreaming up" must always be literary. [Roni-Sue had made a distinction between dreams based on unconscious mental activity, which seemed to her mechanical operations, in contrast with a "dreaming up" activity of consciousness, which seemed to her more creative, allied with art].

Roni-Sue: The more I let it hang out in my mind, the more I see a shuffle machine. I want to say "a mindless sort of thing", grabbing elements back and forth, past to present, combining forms and following rules, insisting, insisting, like the ocean waves. That would be nice, but I think it's more mechanical than that, an essentially impersonal function applied to what is most deeply personal to us, applied to our desires, even if I wonder if our desires are ours anyway.

Barrie: I like when certain thinkers say our thoughts think us, our dreams dream us and I don't feel slighted by "mechanical". "impersonal" (I have a different notion of "personal"). I don't deride them and the process, and, not over-valuing, I think they are important, creative. Whether it's growth or just feels like growth, or creative or just feels like it, one could always ask the same questions when (supposedly) awake/conscious and making art, writing . . .

Roni-Sue: At the same time, it seems that it is precisely here, in what ultimately feels to me like a manifestation of the death drive, that we have the opportunity to create. I don't even really know what I'm saying, but it feels right at this time. Our conscious minds are the creators.

Barrie: If so, it doesn't take from us, it gives to us, enhances, enhances what we are and what we make.

Roni-Sue: If we can settle down and listen and make something of this incessant repetition.

Barrie: It can be helpful to think of it as different each time, and see the difference (an old lesson from thinkers in many fields). Again, it will always be speech, narrative, literary, a gap away from what it was/is.

Roni-Sue: It seems as if it is popular these days to say things like "I like to dream up my patient".

Barrie: Mystifying language, trendy, beware, and note when it's a claim in a discussion and when or whether it actually happens clinically, and the misuses of the so-called vaunted practice of dreaming up.

Roni-Sue: I don't know where I'm going with this other than to wonder what people are really saying when they say that.

Barrie: Me too, and I partially shudder to think. If jargon is fairly new or contemporary, it seems or may be that people rarely are able to say how they're really using it and if it's becoming ossified.

Roni-Sue: I think there should maybe be a different word. The dream-work is stuck and only the reflecting mind has the opportunity to sense densities.

Barrie: Trust, probe, the images, linguistics (e.g., cognates), sounds, formal and structural things, logics and processes of dreams, rather than narrative. Who knows, no one knows when to trust narratives of dreams. The practice of working well with dreams is invented in the moment, especially fresh in person in dialogue face to face, or in self-analysis with creative practices, and not keeping in mind even Bion's "without memory, desire, etc."

Roni-Sue: To make life out of death.

*   *   *

In another post, Roni-Sue continues:

> There seems overwhelmingly implicit in dreams, transference, repetition compulsion a "drive to represent" which can maybe only be satisfied intersubjectively, which developmentally begins in the dyad, but which also becomes the seed of the ability for one to reflect on one's own thoughts. It seems to me that one real moment of hope in our creative capacity, and a possibility to create a future (in the sense of new experience) happens in the unpacking. This is one capacity that psychoanalysis has allowed me to develop in my own life. What allows or obviates a subject's capacity to detect and unpack our psychic densities?
>
> *Barrie*: Touchstones, with a light hand (painting metaphor) when it comes to narrative. Touchstones, touch, gesture, images, sounds, relationships (logical ones), functions, processes, abstractions. very personal.

In other posts, Barrie continues:

> Thinking about dreams yesterday I wrote some notes. I cannot be one thing. Speech makes me be one thing. When I free-associate many things converge as if I had several different dreams simultaneously, not sequentially. To speak this, impossible. To speak, then, is to present as one thing but many things are going on, so anything I say is wrong, not what calls to be said. Phenomenal multi-dreams. Infinite simultaneous dreams. Is the inability to grasp more than two temporary?
>
> In writing a dream I have to make choices. I experience it as a crossroads. [Having to choose a specific mode of expression] interferes with dream flow on to a page because there are two dream flows—if only I could write with two hands at once. I envision the extra hand I need as appended to the same (right) arm. I manage with discomfort writing as fast as I can fragments and inevitably quickly forgetting prime details of twin dreams completely unidentical, and then inferred, implied, infinitely rippled others, vanished . . .
>
> I see my infinite dreams stacked like pancakes or LPs, 45s, 78s over a turntable. But only fleetingly or intermittently. My imagination of them is simultaneously mixed (not exclusive, not either/or, deeply non-binary). I see them flowing (liquid; water or mercury or other viscosities) uncontrollably by the grasping "conscious" mind. That is, or may be, the "mind's" effect on them, as if the infinite dreams are

not part of the mind but grasped at by the mind ("consciousness"). All flowing together with elements that can go any which way and keep moving. It's random, but then I think there "is" purpose—not as arbitrary as watching clouds and reading images into them, but still literary. My repertoire of knowledge or acquaintance of such things as mechanics, electronics, cinema, painting, sound, and image, mediate my impressions of dream workings, and such idiosyncrasies point to history of ideas about dream-work.

I often dream of between-ness. I experience it as emphasising the abstraction, logic, architectural diagram (house, rooms), but then leading me to the abstract between, emotional resonance and impact of between, still mysterious to me but beckoning. Mysterious dreams of between have been pushing through for decades.

I want to add that after these writings, since then, I have realised something about theatre, about theatricality, about how theatricality/theatre perhaps can capture best (not writing with one hand what needs infinite hands) might be what captures/"captures" dreams or gets them all in one package.

* * *

Shomer Zwelling (psychologist in Williamsburg, Virginia, who integrates yoga and meditation in his practice), touched by threads of Barrie's posts, at one point described intertwining dreams like the braids of *challah*, a dream *challah*:

On several nights, this very week, I've been experiencing dreams that seem braided in time during a single phase of sleep. Not exactly simultaneous dreams but when I awake the feel of experiencing a double helix of dreams, a dream *challah*, dreams interwoven, gently swirling, undulating like soft fabrics of story and people in space. The dreams seem to have a similar feel, flow, atmosphere, a dancing relationship, even though the surface content is quite different. Also, different from a dream within a dream; rather, both dreams seemingly independent while also subtly, maybe energetically, in moving relationship, dream fragments dancing in cyberspace.

A few days later, Shomer posted:

Concerning obliterated dream memories—two nights ago I awoke after having two different dream experiences. The first dream seemed like a very long one, an extended thread of scenes, sequencing one to another, including seeing a film in a theatre twice within the dream, once by myself and another time with a friend, and then discussing the film on a walk with the friend, who had her own opinion of the film and saw the film from another perspective, including the fact that she thought the film had another narrator than I did. The second dream I couldn't quite remember, only the presence of the dream remained in conscious, awake memory, as it were an afterglow feeling of the dream, a sensation within my mind of the dream that included vague visual impressions of the dream, dream traces, or maybe traces of traces, soft and slight energy surges or the remains of surges, but I could not see a clear picture of the dream content, let alone find the words for the traces I was experiencing while awake other than a sense of a glowing light in a part of my mind where I felt/knew a dream had transpired. The sensation of the interior glowing light from the dream during wakefulness was pleasurable, but at the same time I also had a melancholic feeling over not being able to fully recall the dream's particular content, the play and interplay of conscious and unconscious processes/experiences.

I am among those who "believe" work takes place within the dream itself as well as afterwards. Along with others, I tend to see the dream as another perspective on lived experience, another perspective and/or glimpse into the experience of being the person/energy field called "Shomer". Sometimes, upon waking, I feel the dream was a fuller manifestation of a particular thought that I only vaguely experienced during the day, and that partially formed thought became more fully expressed during the dream experience at night. For example, the other day I had a vague, uncanny feeling while driving alone on a road linking one shopping centre to another beside a four/six lane highway filled with traffic and lined with shopping malls. The experience passed quickly. I was busy driving to a Chinese restaurant to pick up some take-out food, and I had lots of other immediate, concrete things to do, too. During the night's dream I was on the same curve in the road, but the road itself was in the country and it was a dirt path for cars. Upon waking, I remembered being on that particular dirt road at some point in my life but couldn't precisely place that road, "knew" immediately that the uncanny feeling from the previous day on the curved road had been a reference to the particular dirt road seen and experienced in my dream. In other words, both the dream and the previous day's experience were pointing to yet another lived experience.

Later that same day, I asked my wife to join me for a country walk we often take on a road in the woods that's hardly travelled by cars, and the road includes an additional link like the one in my dream and also like the connecting link during the previous day's driving experience in the shopping centres. The connection of the dream to waking experience still seems slightly out of reach, slightly inaccessible, only the vague feeling of a memory/experience still remains, but in general, while awake, I try to be patient and attuned to the memory traces in something of a meditative, witnessing state, allowing/encouraging as best I can the process to unfold. Perhaps the experience of writing this email and communicating it to you will provide additional support to the process: an ongoing exploration of still silent places where illusive winds and energies subtly swirl and manifest.

*   *   *

The posts made by the three individuals above show the magnetic force dreams exercise and experiential doors they open, sometimes teasingly, sometimes touched by wonder and gratitude or fear and dread. Links are made between waking and sleeping experience, as if a dreaming dimension runs through both. A dreaming dimension felt as real, even more than real, and adds realness to reality. The world becomes more colourful and enticing through dreaming, as if what we call reality is already a dreaming reality, reality made up of dreams, a dream-filled reality. What comes out, too, is the importance of vague feelings as well as clear images. Sometimes, there is an almost evanescent sense of something present, hard to say what. That "vague feeling" itself is an important part of reality, a delicate thread in a largely unknown but valued fabric, filaments of experience with no name or place that quietly thrill, suggest, calm, beckon (Eigen, 2014).

I would say that reality has the power to crush dreams, but dreams themselves often express fears involving loss, invasion, and nameless dreads. Ways in which we feel crushed or mad or worried find paths in our dreams (Eigen, 1986, Chapter Two). There are times when dream and reality seem very far apart, but often they are interwoven, part of each other, not only mutually constitute as separate, but also mutually permeating, made up of each other as well.

Often, we feel or hear of a gap between intimations of a fuller sense of being and the bit of being we live. William Wordsworth wrote of everything once "Apparell'd in celestial light / The glory and the freshness of a dream / It is not now as it hath been of yore / . . . there hath passed away a glory from the earth" ("Intimations of Immortality" from *Recollections in Early Childhood*). The poet writes of radiance that wanes as one grows. Bion also felt that, for the infant, everything is animate, a sense that diminishes with time and development. Freud wrote of a malaise, a discontent, Buddha of *dukka*, a sense of dissatisfaction that is part of life. Complaints of feeling unreal, alienated, meaningless are painful side effects of loss and wounds of living.

Too often, we demand from others the fullness we lack and consequent resentment plays a role in making life even more painful. There is a tendency to spoil experiences because we feel they are not good enough. Some moments are fuller than others. Some are close to maximal, and perhaps there are experiences that ring the bell of bells, super-maximal. We need to learn to traverse ranges of experience along the intensity and fullness spectrum, including daily tasks that need to be done whether semi-fatigued, distracted, enjoying them or not, pushing yourself to get through because existence requires it.

A sense of something missing has been noted since antiquity. As mentioned above, Plato's shadows on the wall of the cave, St Paul's through a glass darkly, St Thomas's beatific vision, Chassidic vision of "the world to come". The Eternal Something More, my cup runneth over. Goodness and mercy over evil and death.

The fact of multi-dimensional continua of experiences varying in intensity and fullness may be basis enough for the nagging sense that there ought to be more. Sometimes, there *is* more and we might formulate a wish that it always be so. Some use drugs to achieve more maximal states more of the time, heightening or soothing states on demand. Some use exercise or art or writing or prayer. But there often is the drop down, the spiritual or aesthetic hangover, pains the next day. Ups and downs of experience, sometimes birth pains.

Winnicott (Eigen, 1993) writes of experience itself as inherently creative, aside from the notion of creativeness that involves products. It might be that art, music, literature, philosophy, religion, politics, and science are more specialised and focused distillations of the intrinsic creativeness of experience. Birth of experience runs through culture *and* everyday life.

A few moments ago, I wrote of everyday life as if it were a second-class citizen, a runner-up to moments of heightened intensity. I feel quite the opposite. There is much in everyday life you simply have to get through. That is part of daily living, of creating a life. But it is also a relief to be just plain you doing things you need to do. Putting yourself into the task at hand can be comforting and fulfilling. Harold Searles would say he liked washing dishes because it soothed him. Well, I think I mean that and more. There is intrinsic satisfaction in jobs well done and seeing to the chores needed to make life possible is itself gratifying, even if some of what you have to do is onerous or boring. Still more, a quiet glow often accompanies pleasures and pains of daily labour. In Judaism, blessings are associated with many daily activities, a sense of the holy in everyday life, miracles of everyday. There are so many ways to use yourself, to be of use, to exercise your life, your capacities.

To exercise and rest. In Taoism, there is also a notion of creative uselessness. The importance of seemingly useless states and activities, aimless moments, time off from oneself. One Taoist example, a tree, limbs and trunk so crooked it cannot be used for anything. It escapes the axe and lives out its useless life providing beauty and shade. Beauty and shade and something more—something about an old tree with limbs doing unexpected things, the knotted bark, a sense of age, of being alive through the ages, of ages alive in you, buried in you, the whole history of the earth buried in you, all of life in your limbs, trunk, roots.

*   *   *

There are many myths of loss, of something missing. Aristophanes wrote of primordial beings cut in half, man–man, man–woman, woman–woman, each half seeking the other in order to feel whole. Perhaps a hint of God being cut in half is buried in hints of a hermaphroditic god, male and female sides. Folklore and gnostic tales speak of the soul coming down from heaven to be born on earth. There are Jewish stories of the soul's shriek in its descent, leaving heaven, entering the womb, sometimes portrayed as north-dry to south-wet. Trauma on both sides of the "fall", leaving and loss, entering the new, blind, unknowing.

And what of womb dramas? Picture the amazing growth of a fertilised egg in nine months, the emergence of organs and functions. If you grew that much with such speed outside the womb, imagine what you might feel. What we must go through in the womb! And yet folklore and psychoanalysis pictured the womb as a kind of perfect heaven, needs met effortlessly, and birth a trauma. Entering or leaving the womb is trauma, depending on which story dominates the moment.

The idea of needs being met effortlessly remains an important image for a thread of existence. The wish for perfect need-fulfilment and a partial attitude that expects or hopes for satisfaction without work, pain, difficulty, or struggle. One hears someone described as wanting to go back to the womb or having never left it. One fears a regressive pull towards nullity. I have had patients who stayed in bed for months. Life was too much, their beings too oppressive. They could not move, had little impetus. In some cases, this inertia over time converted into a more alive womb experience, discovery of need for nourishment, holding, even a need for birth. In the 1960s, I remember therapies based around trying to re-create a sense of being born, perhaps even gestation in the womb. There is a big difference between inert dying out and alive gestation, although both are important experiences. The need not to be and to be intertwine.

I have heard the fact of birth used as an argument for life after death. Just as the foetus might think its experience in the womb is all of existence, not foreseeing worlds to be discovered once hatched, so the dying individual may have no idea of worlds to come. Whether or not there is truth in this analogy, I think it expresses a powerful template of experience. The idea of being born applies to psychological and spiritual birth as well.

There are many wombs to leave. For some people, more intensely and impossibly than others. I have had patients who could not go to school as children. Several feared terrible things would happen, such as being kidnapped, if they left the protection of the home. In some instances, one cannot go outside.

The biblical Jacob was described as staying in the tent with his mother, while his brother Esau was an outdoors man, a hunter, perhaps a womaniser. A mother's son and a father's son. What was Jacob doing in the tents? Cooking and studying *Torah* (the Eternal *Torah*, since the literal one had not yet been given to Moses). In *The Psychoanalytic Mystic* (1998), I describe Jacob as undergoing a more complex process of invagination than Esau, a more complex development, perhaps one meaning of "more life", the blessing his father was tricked into giving him. One can see a parallel between Jacob and Esau and the rich inward steeping of Abel and the impulsive Cain, although both tendencies need development. We live in and with inner–outer worlds which require varied kinds of learning. Jacob and Esau represent different birth processes with developmental trajectories, aspects of our multi-dimensional development.

Birth, as well as death, anxiety goes on all life long. Some children who could not play outside or go to school had severe difficulties shedding the skin or shell of childhood as puberty and adolescence required further kinds of birth. There is no one response to this difficulty. Often, dread of suffocation and the need to cling go together. As the child grows to teenage years, extremes of withdrawal and impulsiveness can occur. Withdrawal as part of the need for protection and succour, impulsiveness to break free of it and feel more independent—often both ends working against the other. As college or work loom, new sets of birthing invite and threaten. I have worked with many young people lost in a sea of life too large to swim in, unable to find the traction that birth requires. Failures of birth can happen at any phase of development, transitioning in–out of house, school, adolescence, college, beyond. To learn how to be born and born again spans levels of existence.

Lacan uses the image/reality of the placenta as an entry into a sense of loss that goes with extra-uterine life. He links loss of the placenta with loss of a sense of immortality, deathlessness, and the necessary realisation of mortality, death, perhaps somewhat parallel to William Blake's *Songs of Innocence* and *Songs of Experience*. A loss of an organ and a time in which nutrition, waste, and gas exchange was mediated through the mother's blood. One, perhaps, imagines a wholeness that does not exist.

To what extent is wholeness a fantasy or wish or taste of momentary states that endure in memory and form part of a background of experiential possibilities? One does, indeed, experience varied qualities of existence, feeling some are better than others, from anguish to bliss. Inner scales, not only of pleasure–pain, but also of joy–dread, become part of a background texture and taste of life, an open reservoir of possibilities informing psychic taste buds.

Perhaps positing a wholeness that gets split into halves or parts seeking each other does not take into account what it felt like to be a pre-split being. It is unlikely, on the plane of *Malchut*, planet earth, that any state can be without difficulties for long, although some are more heavenly than others. Apparently God felt Adam in the Garden lacked something to begin with ("It is not good for man to be alone"). The story of division gives some kind of expression to perturbations in paradise. In a purely homogeneous field, it is unlikely our world could have begun.

* * *

As a young man, I first came across the term "primordial experience" in writings on myth and spirituality and then found resonances in depth psychology. Even the words "primordial experience" have a ring of depth, differentiating everyday life from a deeper, fuller dimension, perhaps foundational dimensions underlying and inform-ing the surface of things. I read Jung before Freud, loved them both. For some time, Jung's sense of the primordial made me feel at home, linking psychology and myth with deep unconscious life. I felt creative resonance as deep as I could go, something, in its own way, to which Kabbalah gives expression. As St Augustine wrote, follow-ing the psalms, "Wherever I go, You are there." Although Jung charted basic structures of the unconscious, I also related to its in-finity, endlessness (something Bion emphasises, 1994; Eigen, 2012a).

Out of hosts of possibilities, I am choosing to emphasise some elements of Henry Elkin's writings (1972; Eigen, 1986, 2004). He was an anthropologist, trained as a Jungian in Switzerland, moved towards Freud, assimilated Klein, Winnicott, and was reading Bion and Lacan towards the end of his life. He also had exposure to vari-ous kinds of body work and was part of the existential psychology movement. He hoped to develop a theory in which positive findings of the various schools of depth psychology could be situated.

Elkin posits a primordial phase of development in which the infant does not yet have clear space–time awareness (in what we later call "realistic" terms) or cognition of materiality and embodiment. It takes time to develop a self and body image with a realisation that one, so to speak, must be where one's body is. Elkin feels an infant experi-ences consciousness and self-awareness before developing a clear sense of material embodiment.

Elkin divides the primordial stage into two phases: the first charac-terised by pre-consciousness or consciousness, sentience, awareness, vital sensing, and the second with fuller, emergent awareness that it is I or me or self that is sensing. One senses, is aware. In time, "I" sense, am aware, and am aware of myself. Elkin sketches emergence of self-awareness from awareness as such.

Kurt Koffka (1963) wrote of a mountain climber's fall that left him unconscious. When he began coming to, he experienced a field of awareness and, after a time, became aware that it was he who was aware, the I growing out of a field of consciousness. Federn (1957) noted processes of depersonalisation, loss of I-feeling in states moving towards psychosis. He described many variations of I-feeling, even to the point of suggesting that part of some psychoses is not being able to get the I into the body, a refusal of, or incapacity for, embodiment. One can go further and say there are states in which one refuses, or is unable, to squeeze oneself into an I or self, not only body. Of course, there are no pure states, everything is mixed with varying emphases and organisations.

One can give many instances in which consciousness goes on ticking with or without I-awareness, important as the latter is. Elkin goes further, saying that it takes time to build a picture of the material aspect of the world, to learn the limitations of the space one occupies. And prior to cognising materiality, one lives in a world of ineffable, more total experience. Not all the time, perhaps, but enough of the time to lay down templates of positive and negative infinities.

Elkin feels the baby laughing or smiling, associated with face recognition at a distance, somewhere around two or three months (according to data he had at the time he wrote), signalled the growth of primordial self and other awareness, a kind of self-to-self experience. The body is a feeling body, expressive body, part of a feeling ambience, and one tunes in, feelings-to-feelings, the latter becoming part of self–other dramas.

Elkin charts a momentous drama with birth of self-awareness, including miraculous apprehension of one's psychic reality, awareness of one's existence, incipient psychical subject and object to oneself. I suspect much goes on implicitly in the phase of primordial pre-consciousness/consciousness that begins to become more explicit and undergoes development in the phase of primordial self-awareness. At the outset of primordial self-awareness, Elkin depicts a kind of initial Buddha-like consciousness surrounded by a benign void that is hit by disturbance, say, stomach pains, change of temperature, other felt attacks. The benign primordial surround becomes menacing, attacking, and the emergent self becomes fearful or rageful to offset the fear. The primordial self feels threatened by a hostile or indifferent primordial other. The pristine, benign self and other give way to a threatened, agonised self in the face of insensitivity, neglect, attack. Images of demons or witches reflect the latter experience. Elkin depicts this aspect of the drama as an intermediate phase too many become stuck in, all this taking place on a feeling plane, without clear recognition of material boundaries, infinities of feeling, moment to moment. The pain can be unbearable and, if not relieved, the infant can lose awareness of self, blot out, a kind of stupor.

The culminating phase of primordial self–other drama occurs when help comes and the agony is relieved enough for self to reappear, a rebirth, the primordial other mediating a sense of divine mercy, goodness, support, foundation for trust and faith. Emergent self-awareness traverses a range of experiences, through hell, the valley of death, and resurrection, with concurrent experiences of the boundless other as demonic and divine.

* * *

As development towards a clearer sense of embodied self and other continues, primordial self-awareness gives way to emergent ego structures and enduring organisations of experience. Background memories or intimations of near total, absolute affective–perceptual states going through demonic–divine dramas implicitly remain, but time–space dramas begin to replace ineffable infinity states, although both meld and have trajectories throughout life. It is as if primordial self-awareness is refracted into various ego structures with characteristic affective attitudes, including autistic, schizoid, paranoid, hysterical, collective, and personal–communal ego structures.

In a more embodied, spatially distinct realm, one becomes more aware of power dimensions, for example, the mother's greater size and strength, the infant's attempt to manipulate it, states of compliance, giving in, resentment, suppression of aggression together with impulse outbursts. Hiding and dissociation militate against total going through affective moments that characterised primordial life. In primordial life, nothing was held back. The infant went through its states, no holds barred. Now, subterfuge becomes a stronger part of the human condition. As things go on, one learns inner tricks necessary to get one's way or to attempt to minimise traumatic aspects of one's situation. One enters "reality" as we come to know it. Sometimes, I get an image of a telescope progressively unfolding, on one end the larger, fuller base, with successive contractions towards the tip through which the eye focuses. A goal of therapy, perhaps, is to assimilate various split-off ego attitudes—paranoid, autistic, schizoid, hysteric, collective—into a larger, personal–communal framework.

Much is gained through development and much lost. Loss is necessary for growth, yet compensations are many. One thing that tends to be lost is the full—something like total, absolute—affective states one goes through as an infant. While Wordsworth is rightly nostalgic about loss of celestial infinity glows, he omits the horrific moments of early life, affective horrors with no names or frame of reference that become one's being for a time.

Rumi, the thirteenth century Persian poet and Sufi mystic, is right to suggest we become hosts to the coming and going of affective states, guests in our psychic house. As adults we might feel a nostalgia for what was lost in our need to survive and prosper. For some, it becomes a necessity to tune into intimations of affective life set aside or lost and begin to birth fuller playgrounds of existence. Rumi's saying, "Beyond ideas of right and wrong, there is a field—I'll meet you there", hints of recovering–unconvering–tasting a bit of infant life that now might add rather than drown, as one discovers how to relate to our affective capacity in new ways.

Psychoanalysis enriches the idea that missing elements we so long for have to do with fullness of affective experience in infancy that naturally diminishes as development proceeds. Not a myth of a whole being cut in half, or a soul once one with God in heaven now journeying in planet earth (*Malchut*), although these mythic stories give expression to significant feeling, but the idea that we once went through something approaching absolute affective states of various colours, expressed in later experience and words such as "dire agony, ghastly dread, tremendous awe, sublime bliss" (Elkin, 1972)—states that fade into the background as development unfolds. States that fade into the background, yet colour foreground experience for better and worse.

*   *   *

We continue to be born all life long. Can we learn to mediate better births? In *Coming Through the Whirlwind* (1992), I have a chapter on rebirth that includes deformed, monstrous rebirths. One can be reborn as a monster as well as a better being. Like dreams, most rebirths are aborted. Often attempts at rebirth are responses to catastrophe. Bion notes that a sense of catastrophe can cement a life together. Attempts to work with catastrophe through rebirth often bear the marks of the former.

A young man consulting me felt "unhatched" (his word) in life. In some way, he felt like an unborn chick who failed to come out of the egg. The extra push he imagined necessary was missing. He went through the stages life made him go through, feeling somehow unformed, distant, not quite a bell jar (Plath, 1963) or caul (Freud's Wolf Man), but some kind of veil of distance. He also felt the distance provided a mask. He could try to act "cool" while feeling further and further away.

He attributed the fact of being a good dancer to having distance from what he did (I once heard Fred Astaire remark about the distance he had from his dancing that made the moves he made possible. He felt that with this distance he could create an illusion of flexibility). Dancing was part of my patient's "cool", but not something he could keep up for long in ordinary discourse. He was afraid that if his distance diminished, stuff would pop out that he would regret, stuff that would spoil the imperturbable, confident, together, benign image he hoped to create.

At the same time, hiding behind his image was costly. He felt he was missing out on life and often slipped into private states of disorganisation. He was afraid if people knew him as he was, he would not be liked. A deeper realisation was that he did not like himself. The split that "saved" him deprived him of himself. He felt risking "hatching" would be too messy and the outcome uncertain. He might end up worse than now. I do not blame the young man for being fearful of risking his "front" for something unknown. As often is the case in therapy, one is caught in seemingly unsolvable dilemmas.

I agreed that being born could be a bloody, messy business, and recalled that Bion, in a session with me, remarked on the "nasty business" of becoming oneself. The table was set, now for the dinner.

*   *   *

In psychosis and psychotic-like states, individuals can be gripped, possessed, by negative states that threaten to ruin their lives. For some, demons or the Devil himself. Attempts to reach areas of health are met by images and voices that threaten eternal damnation. For some, rebirth processes activate annihilation dreads and, with steps forward, one is thrown back into horror. No easy answer, but patient, open work, coming back time and again to the negative moment and coming through it as one can.

One psychoanalytic school I attended taught that with serious psychoses, no real gain can be expected before five years. I sometimes "joke" with supervisees, when the latter are beset with seemingly intractable problems, that things may look a little different in ten or fifteen years. Unless emergency threatens, a worker needs open-ended, unrushed time to be there and keep being there. I am fond of Bion remarking, in response to Macbeth's asking the physician, "Canst thou not minister to a mind diseased?", "Not now, but come back in two hundred years and we'll see." Well, one never knows when two hundred years or the world to come will be. Never, or the next moment? It is serious and severe work, picking oneself up moment after devastating moment, regrouping, reworking. Therapy as an extended crisis of faith; faith as background of birth.

In *Toxic Nourishment* (1999), I present cases that go on and on. Yet, something happens over time, hard to describe. Sometimes, I sense it as a kind of affective attitudinal transmission, a new frame of reference for emotional life gradually birthing, in which good feeling has more room to breathe, no longer fully succumbing to bad, although attacks can happen at any time. More good or better moments come into existence with chance to grow. That does not mean the devil will not do its work or that chronic background self-hate and lack of worth is ineffective. But something more has been added to the brew, a difference that makes a difference.

* * *

For Bion, dreaming played a role in condensing, storing, narrating, digesting experience, also a role in repair and discovery, in so far as alpha dream-work is operating in the mix. He felt dream-work goes on twenty-four hours a day in various ways. He also felt dream-work can become broken, damaged. In one case, by trying to process what cannot be processed, or, at least, what cannot be processed at a given time, for example, an emotionally charged image or object that is too horrifying. Like seeing Medusa or God and dying, dream-work becomes damaged under the strain of trying to digest what is, as yet, beyond digestion, akin to living in a chronic state of emotional indigestion (Eigen, 1998, 2001b). Many dreams are aborted dreams, as the affect a dream works with might be too much for it and it breaks off. Similarly, many rebirths are aborted or partial births, the psycho-organism lacking capacity for more.

Dreams often try to do many things at once: for example, they try to work creatively with emotional problems that might seem insoluble, give expression to painful dilemmas, psychic sore spots and stuck spots, wounds and blocks in dealing with them, and they can be a kind of SOS, cries of pain, semi-paralysed signals of catastrophe (Eigen, 1986).

I think there are different kinds of dreams and dream processes or, at least, different emphases. Although dreams may be repetitive, they also have a chance to contribute something new or take things further. They can keep imaging a stuck point, but often with a sense of striving to open a path or, at least, chip off a bit from the density that can undergo some processing. Some dreams contribute towards problem solving and creation of new experience or nuances of experience.

When alpha dream-work is working well (i.e., when dream-work is in an alpha function mode and alpha is relatively undamaged), it can contribute to furthering experience more quickly and effectively than simply conscious work. The two together—conscious and unconscious processes—form a team when working well, but if something is wrong with unconscious transmission, consciousness can become stingy. The two naturally undergo continua of states and relationships along contraction–expansion dimensions that can get stuck, congeal, freeze in ways that require attention.

Freud sometimes was at a loss as to what to call the "consciousness" felt at work unconsciously. He adopted the term "unconscious", which was common in his time, but added further meaning to it. Many capacities work unconsciously, some going in and out of consciousness. Freud drew attention to unconscious erotic, impulsive pressures, but also pressures of conscience, as if the two were counterparts of each other. Many ego processes bent on survival of the individual in the face of inner–outer pressures also functioned unconsciously as well as consciously. In his earlier work, there were dramatic tensions between racial and individual survival needs as well. His work contains riveting dramas between psychic functions and conscious–unconscious work. For me, reading him (or Jung), like Kabbalah, makes me feel all the more what amazing capacities we have, along with difficulties in learning to use them.

Freud called the "id" (It) the true psychical reality—the primary psychical reality. One could sense resonance between Freud's emphasis on the unconscious as a primary psychical reality and Elkin's depiction of primordial experience as substructure. Both tune into a domain of being deeper than everyday surface reality. Freud felt the id was out of contact with the external world and other structures (ego, I) evolved under the latter's impact. Freud noted similarities between id and "old brain", emotional brain, and ego with cortical functions, a linkage which has been carried forward with more complex research tools in recent times.

There is something about out of contact and in-contact elements that strikes emotional, phenomenological chords. Although we are now pretty well schooled in field theory, and sense that self–other grow up together, mutually constitutive, there is still something about the notion of being out of contact or in contact that is important. Such states inform each other, intertwine, dissociate, reconfigure in many ways. Poets and film-makers use an array of images to evoke versions of these tendencies, to be in and out of contact at the same time or sequentially. The terms "contact barrier" and "contact function", as used in psychoanalysis, in part reflect concern with problematic aspects of making, keeping, losing contact with aspects of oneself or others or the world. We ought not to use views of the moment to seal possibilities or think we know more than we do. A lot of surprises are likely to lie ahead.

In the last decades of his life, Freud added a death drive to the unconscious and what we might call death-work. He meant to contrast it with life drive, the former building unities, the latter undoing them, akin to metabolic–catabolic processes. Informally, he linked with Moses's final, or near final, concern, wondering whether the human race will choose life or death. The death drive came to be allied with destruction, a destructive urge, although theory and reality are more complicated. Bion envisioned a tendency in human life to undo everything, perhaps partly a claustrophobic reaction in response to feeling hemmed in by one's makeup, personality, identity, and products. One might even feel that the death drive can have a positive function, creative destruction. Not only in clearing out the old and making room for the new, but a tendency towards zero, no-thing, emptiness, a null point that can act as a birth pond, no-place to start over. A positive, creative aspect of being no one nowhere, for moments free of oneself, free of being and non-being.

Bion emphasised a permanently embryonic aspect of personality, akin to Tao's unborn, so that more birth is possible. Imagine plus and minus zero states, linked to better and worse births, fused. Bion remarked that life is filled with surprises, most of them bad. He also felt that a child's playing session often ends in tears. But the negative does not preclude the new. Drops of unexpected experience can sometimes be squeezed out of pain. Emergence of self and other can give rise to a generative background sense of life. Similarly, pain and joy combine like parental couples making psychic babies in so many ways, not always what one hoped, sometimes more than one hoped, but what one has to work with.

*   *   *

Bion's work straddles many worlds at once, giving expression to a sense that we *are* many worlds at once, a vision that is part of Kabbalah. How many models can dance on the head of an affect? Sometimes, I think of Bion as a philosophical psychoanalyst or psychoanalytic philosopher, but these labels do not quite work. He seeks contact with psychic reality, at the same time being aware that maps are not the realities they depict. Even dreams are selective narratives, organised expressions of emotional nuclei that remain largely unknown and guessed at. We may have information about how we organise and depict experience, but experience as such remains slippery. We cannot even say that what we say is inaccurate, since we lack ability to know to what extent it is accurate or not. We work with pictures and intimations, sometimes feeling they are closer to points of contact than others. Bion is not willing to give up reality or give up on it. Emotional life is real and we live it, although representations of it may be lacking.

Bion emphasises the selective aspect of all narratives, which inherently "biases" stories about ourselves. Alpha function, to which he assigns tasks of storage, digestion, and processing emotional life, necessarily works in partial ways, chewing on bits of emotive impacts as it can. Yet, its slants on experience, through a glass darkly, are part of experience it tries to work with. An inevitable circle, perhaps, but one we live with and seek to learn more about. A Zen "cartoon" I saw showed an insect in a jar. Over and over the insect tried to get out, but fell back even after heroic attempts. In the last frame, you see the insect appreciatively examining his condition, at once looking at the jar and looking out, saying, "Nice jar."

By touching the fact of uncertainty, Bion calls for humility that leaves space for further possibilities. He speaks of the importance of unsaturated space, space unsaturated by meaning. One can overdo meaning, drowning out aspects of experiencing with meaning floods, missing something still deeper, something more creative. Over-saturating with meaning does not leave room for meaning. These and similar facts are not problems to be solved, but conditions of existence. As I wrote earlier, you might view the dream as a shadow cast by emotional reality and our interpretations shadows cast by the dream.

*   *   *

I noted the possibility of creative aspects of a death drive or zero tendency, perhaps beyond nothing and emptiness. Bion wrote of a force that goes on destroying after it destroys everything, feeding on destruction itself (Eigen, 1998). He seems to have meant it as a negative tendency that is part of us, which we can meet only with faith, the psychoanalytic attitude. But there is perhaps also a death moment beyond destruction or beyond our destructive activity. Death that enlarges us the closer it comes.

I remember an early taste of this when I was thirty, holding my aunt's hand as she was dying, unable to tell when life left off and death began. A further moment and I could not tell the difference between life and death, they were one. This was not an expected experience or an intellectual exercise. It just happened. Suddenly, it was reality, something new opened. When I left, I realised my fear of death, so acute throughout my twenties, had disappeared. Not that it was gone forever, but something decisive occurred. My chest, arms, legs relaxed, expanded. All at once I had become a fuller being.

At times, when death is near, I feel something like velvet or silk curtains, an inexpressibly soft touch. But there are moments when death presses more grimly, matter of fact. I think over my life, crises, choice points, all you have to swallow to get along with yourself and others. We swallow a lot of death in order to live. And sometimes, Roni-Sue Allen adds, we allow ourselves to be swallowed in order to survive.

Death opens new digestive capacities and more, realities deeper than words can reach, in which digestion becomes less relevant. I would like to stress a mysteriously enriching aspect, as if a kind of invisible ink of experience becomes palpable, a new form of ineffable touch, veil after veil.

It is beyond the velvety, silky feeling I mentioned before. It is hard to say where you feel it. Sometimes, a kind of chest feeling, as if my chest has "fingers", "feelers" that sightlessly spread throughout. Another kind of chest, beyond treasure chest, no location you can pin down—impalpable palpable. Death, here, becomes part of Grace.

*　*　*

The death-as-grace moment described above comes unpremeditated. One does not work for it. It happens, takes one by surprise, opens reality. One can, over time, live one's way into this dimension, explore it, get to "know" it (perhaps via *Daat* as perception: "You favour man with perception"—*Shemoneh Esreh*, Jewish prayer).

This contrasts with depths of pain and struggle. For example, a moment in the *Seder* when the Hebrew slaves cry out and God hears their cry and takes them out of Egypt with a strong, outstretched arm. Not an angel, not a messenger, God Himself.

This is followed by the journey through the wilderness, working on ourselves in varying degrees and ways, struggling with ourselves. Many crises of faith occur, struggling with faith and life. Moses as emblem of struggle leading to meeting God at Mount Sinai, followed by further struggle mediating laws and working with difficulties approaching the Holy Land. And still further hardships and painful realities associated with entrance to the Holy Land outside and the Holy Land within.

I take this story to be a way of speaking about an inner journey towards a shift of being, a portrayal of different dimensions of being: (1) a slave state and psychology, often needed for learning to work hard, exertion, apprenticeship; (2) purifying struggle with oneself; (3) God-meeting, dimensions of Grace; (4) actualising Grace, heaven within keeps opening, some of it touching the world. A kind of heavenly drip combined with human struggle.

*　*　*

Struggle comes in many forms. Rank (1932) focused on a relentless creative urge that uplifts and opens existence; at the same time, it can have destructive consequences for the personal life of an artist. Rank felt the struggle between art and life was unresolvable, that an individual must choose one or the other. I am not so sure this must always be the case. I tend to look for avenues of mutual nourishment between capacities. But Rank makes a strong case for a trade-off, at least areas of trade-off, between life and art. Absorption in art militated against living a fuller "personal" life. In part, Rank portrayed art as symbiotic—perhaps parasitic—on life, drawing on your life, using your resources, giving you something while sucking you dry. Jung, too, gave as example the poet turning his life into words (poets have a high rate of suicide and early death). Bion wrote of creativity greed and a state of mind that can veer towards madness or creativeness or both. Wolfgang Kohler (Henle, 1971) wrote of the necessary obsessiveness that went with creativity, as the latter pressed towards finding or "solving" problems, exploring materials and sets of variables that captivate and egg one on.

A symbiosis and war between art and life. Will the latter use the former or the former the latter? Can both thrive together? It is a question that haunted me in work with psychosis. Arieti (1974, 1976) and Bettelheim(1961) wrote about a trade-off between apparent creativeness and health. Schizophrenic patients in earlier phases of therapy showed more creative thinking and experiencing, leaps of images and thoughts that seemed to undergo burnout as the person got better, as if creativity was sacrificed as madness diminished, enabling a better life. Is this necessary? I do not think so but there is no question that for many people it happens. In *Flames From the Unconscious: Trauma, Madness, and Faith* (2009), I tried to delineate processes in which creativity went along with more life as individuals got better (no more hospitalisations and, for some, becoming medication free as well). It is an issue I have been discussing since my first book on psychosis (1986). There is much individual variation and no one answer. Rank homes in on what creativity demands of the artist and wonders if life can sustain it. He zeroes in on an intense creativity drive that was implicitly central for Freud and explicitly for Bion (who calls creativity, along with murder and parasitism, a basic tropism).

My reading of Rank in the 1960s had a strong impact. I determined not to let creativity ruin my life, whether as writer or analyst. It took a long time to try to find a way to live out some of my creativity at the same time as becoming a devoted family man. It is not easy straddling worlds. There is a tension between creativity and family living that does not ever get "resolved" or, rather, must be re-solved over and over. Winnicott's formulation of living being creative, primary creativity inherent in living, not just "producing", was a foil or balance to creative elitism (I contrast Freud's and Winnicott's views on creativity in *The Electrified Tightrope*, 1993).

A similar tension characterises a vein of religious experience, in which celibacy is contrasted with family life and sexuality. St Paul concludes that family life is second best. One can get closer to God by dedicating all one's capacities to spiritual service, but family life is better than "burning" (not just in hell, but in sexual tension). In contrast, for me, family life might be one of the most important enrichments of spirituality I could have known. The challenges to personal development that family life presents can add enormously to what it is possible to experience and learn. We are gifted with amazing capacities that can take so many forms. As our external world has so many contrasts, bursting with possibilities, so does human personality.

* * *

Fairbairn (1954) gives us another idea of inner struggle, in part struggle with the environment, in part within ourselves. The struggles he depicts necessarily involve shifts in structures of experiencing, closely allied, but not identical, with phenomenology, as if in order to handle trauma, the personality reinvents itself and reinvents itself again.

Something that has puzzled analysts is Fairbairn's writing that a good object—in contrast with Melanie Klein—is not internalised. It simply is lived, real. Klein (1946) suggests we internalise a good object core as well as bad objects, and the former helps offset the force of the latter (tied as the latter are, for her, with the death drive and annihilation anxiety). Her account seems to include double psychic nuclei— good and bad objects—from near the beginning (Eigen, 1998, 2007).

For Fairbairn, internalisation comes about to help mitigate trauma. Global traumatic impact is broken into component parts. He emphasises two main elements, excitement–rejection and depicts the global trauma object being broken into two objects, exciting and rejecting objects. To effect this, the ego breaks into component parts, a libidinal ego tied to the exciting object and anti-libidinal ego tied to the rejecting object. He describes this as a divide and conquer technique, ego components dissociating and partly sacrificing themselves to take the wind out of full traumatic impact, but leaving personality subject to shifting winds of excitement–rejection dramas. New personality structures grow in the face of difficulty, but, rather than transcend the problem, reinstate it as part of the structure of personality. One partly becomes the trauma one seeks to master. Personality remains unconsciously subject to structures that arose to diminish traumatic impact. It is, therefore, not simply trauma that is at stake but ways one unconsciously sought to handle it. Fairbairn referred to therapy as a kind of exorcism, in which dissociated ego structures and their objects are drawn out and worked with, aiming to moderate personality dissociations.

Another way of envisioning this involves reintegrating libidinal and anti-libidinal ego components, at least partly, with a central ego that remains in contact with reality. For Fairbairn, unlike Klein, the central ego does not rely on an internalised good object for support— it gets its support from good objects in reality. Real, good experience is what nourishes the central ego. This strikes me as an important difference from Klein. The latter relies on an internalised good ego-object to offset bad objects. For Fairbairn, it is direct contact with reality that does the job, contact with validating experience. Really good experience enables growth of the central ego and the possibility of modulating dissociations. You would not ask whether Buber's I–You (Thou) moment is or is not internalised. The moment itself opens new possibilities of reality.

I would not want to have to choose between Fairbairn and Klein. I find both valuable. They touch different aspects of experience and process. I suspect one can develop a framework to integrate the contributions of both, without short-circuiting either. Each tunes in to valuable areas of psychic life, giving emphasis to overlapping but different areas of struggle.

Fairbairn's emphasis on a tripartite ego structure tends to stop with two major dissociative moves. Anti-libidinal ego tied to persecutory/rejecting object is his version of aspects of Freud's superego. And libidinal ego tied to an exciting object is his version of aspects of Freud's id. While Klein has a few major structures, she also writes of the importance of the proliferation of splitting of ego, affect, drive, object. One result of the proliferation of personality splitting is diffusion of affect, loss of feeling. Fairbairn, too, feels the dissociations he describes are defences against further fragmentation, loss of self-and-reality feeling. I might be wrong, but one gets from Klein a profound sense of the devastation splitting can lead to, whereas Fairbairn tends to emphasise its positive function of staving off further fragmentation. This does not mean Fairbairn's view lacks resources to depict the worst. He writes of the schizophrenic feeling his love is bad, while the depressive feels his hate is bad. But, in each case, the personality seems to have more organised resources than the further fragmentation Klein sometimes confronts.

In 1968, I met with Winnicott. We discussed many things (Eigen & Govrin, 2008) and, as I was leaving, he gave me a bunch of books, one of them Fairbairn's. I gave the Fairbairn back, as I already had it and read it. He told me how much he valued it, especially some of the chapters. At the time of our meeting, Winnicott had already written the "use of object" paper, but it did not come out until a year later (1969). Had I known that paper, I would have immediately seen an overlap between Fairbairn and Winnicott and why Winnicott valued Fairbairn. In his use of object account (Eigen, 1981, 1993, 2012b, 2013) Winnicott distinguishes between internalisation processes at work in object relating and something different in object usage, a kind of use of materials from the other's personality in new ways, creative use of interactions beyond internalisation work for growth purposes: a sector or group of processes Fairbairn, had he still been alive, would have found of great interest. It is almost as if Winnicott, in part, furthered an aspect of Fairbairn's work by distilling ways in which one made creative use of other personalities without (or in addition to) introjecting them. It is as if Fairbairn, Winnicott, and Bion felt trapped by internal representations and sought ways to go beyond them. There are many qualification and complexities, but I wish to signal an important thread with which three very creative workers engaged. For both Bion and Winnicott, at least, creativity was an explicit theme.

*   *   *

Bion distinguishes between conscious and becoming conscious. This is a little like the *Zohar* saying, "There is a rose and there is a rose!" (Matt, 2004, Vol. 1, Chapter One). We are conscious of all sorts of things and feelings. Registration happens, but for the registration to become part of living memory for a living being, something more is needed. What is needed for registration to become living memory, available for creative experiencing? One almost tastes parts of processes involved in Ingmar Bergmann's *Wild Strawberries*, where memories of a life come alive. Or Kafka: "I am a memory come alive." For Kafka and Bergmann, moments that come alive are crucial even if in these moments deadness comes alive.

I think this is one of the meanings of so many references of coming alive after feeling dead in the Bible. One dies out with God's absence and comes alive with Presence. A sequence noted over and over, one I call a rhythm of faith (Eigen, 2004). I was dead, now I live. Charting a spiritual–emotional barometer, more alive, more dead (Eigen, 1996, 1998). A sequence with deep roots, mimicking night–day, darkness–light, loss and return of primordial awareness (see earlier section on Elkin, 1972). As mentioned earlier, states of feeling spanning high–low, empty–full, alive–dead are basic affective nuclei in biblical writing and widespread in culture.

Husserl writes of thoughts or feelings needing thinking and feeling and Bion of thoughts in search of a thinker. Perhaps we might speak of a psyche in need of an experiencer, one who appreciates, wrestles with, and is nourished by what being a psychical being offers. One cannot take for granted that because one is a conscious or psychical being that one is a *conscious* or *psychical* being. One may fail to grow into what is offered.

*   *   *

Many years ago, I read that where psychic life is concerned, there are, strictly speaking, no contradictions, although there can be and often is conflict. Part of the way I understood this is that contradiction is a logical concept. In a logical system, you can postulate x contradicts y. But, in reality, x and y not only may coexist, but also be part of each other. X and y may be contradictory in logical propositions, but in art they may supplement and support each other. Art harmonises what logic finds contradictory, although here I might be illegally crossing realms. But that, too, might be part of what I am saying, since hybrid cross-fertilisation may surprise.

What might appear contradictory in logic might be food for mystical experience. You might say there are ways that Freud translated aspects of mystical and creative experience psychologically. Objects, affects, and pronouns fuse, reverse, conflict, nourish. I hate you can be I love you. You hate me can be you love me. Love can be hate and hate can be love. I can be you and you can be me (Eigen, 1986). Freud opens fields of the possible by recognising the operations imagination takes for granted. Metaphor fuses differences and similarities that enhance each other in new unions. Displacement separates in space or time, condensation fuses.

In emotional life, I am alive and I am dead may coexist, describe states or parts of states or mixtures. One can be psychically dead and alive at the same time or experience these states consecutively, dead in some ways, alive in others, more alive now, dead later. One can feel torn apart by states one cannot make room for. One often is pushed to decide between feelings and play down realisation that alternate experiences and views on experience coexist.

To try to give expression to states might result in statements that sound like propositions, but they do not insist on exclusion. Expressive statements try to communicate to oneself or others aspects of psychic reality.

An example of statements that seem like propositions but are expressive of states are: I am. I am not.

As noted, states may conflict but are not contradictory. States that appear to conflict might actually be paradoxical. I am and am not is a statement expressive of states that can and do coexist within a single individual. More, I am and am not may vary and form continua of states of a sense of more or less existence.

Bion remarks, a thing can only be if it is and is not at the same time.

In *Psychic Deadness* (1996), I portray a vast array of states involving a sense of being more dead or alive in varied circumstances and conditions. Perhaps we are not in a realm of contradiction, but one of paradoxical monism (Eigen, 1998).

Much as I like Hegel, and much as there is to get from him if you can, I am not sure about the march of consciousness. To be conscious is not to be good. Consciousness often is deceitful. Bion: lying is ubiquitous.

I remember a debate years ago as to whether a liar can be psychoanalysed. My feeling was, if not who can, given that a liar is also doing the analysing.

When one looks at clinical realities "contradiction" fades, complexity grows. Trauma, for example, can have double effects, depending on variable factors. Trauma can devastate a life and make you stronger, even more creative. Many creative people have a history of extreme experiences. Once a desert guide told my wife and me, looking at a cactus—if not for wounds, the cactus would grow straight, it branches out where it is wounded.

Toxic Nourishment portrays both ends of the spectrum and the middle, including those devastated who do not recover fully and those who must go more deeply to find creative ways to use their sensitivity. Wherever we look, there are spectrums of possibilities. Dogmatism can be an enemy of reality, unable to bear troubling but potentially freeing complexities.

Here is one example of creative thinking trying to envision the birth of an infant's smile, the smile that comes when viewing mother at a distance rather than close. In this vision, the work of paradox gives rise to a smile. Elkin (1972) thought the two-month (or whatever time it might be) smiling response to a face or face representation might involve paradoxical perception of contrast between near–far. The close mother, skin to skin, enfolding when feeding now the far mother, no skin contact, no touch, vision at a distance, eye contact rather than skin contact. Near–far, touch–no touch. A new kind of recognition—the near mother is the far mother, the far mother is the near mother—brings laughter of delight. An elemental happening, a basic sense we have of close–far, touch–no touch.

Meditate on feeling no touch after feeling touch. Does a spiritual sense arise? What does not touching feel like? What is it like to see the other and see the other seeing and responding to one's seeing without skin touching. Sometimes, when I reflect on what this feels like, it is like stepping into another dimension—look ma, no hands. Ineffable "touch" without touch, a new kind of touch from eye-to-eye contact, self-to-self, feeling to feeling. A sense that has a history all life long, dramas of closeness–distance, including intimacy of distance and fog of touch, the positives and negatives of each. We are paradoxical beings who thrive on contrast and reversal, among the varied operations that enable us to still be here, giving flexibility to persistence.

Another set of semi-paradoxical meanings clings to the term "hospitality". I do not know whether or not the multiple meanings, uses, contexts it serves rise to paradox or not. But it comes close to basic quandary sayings such as, to find yourself you must lose yourself, and the concomitant quip, you have to have a self to lose. Levinas and Derrida, particularly, were hospitable to this term, especially in later work. One may be taken aback by the sounding of faith in late Derrida writings and their almost biblically, prophetic insistence.

Husserl and Heidegger are necessary background pivots for Levinas and Derrida, and Merleau-Ponty is in the brew. The term difference, so important to Derrida (1978; Derrida & Dufourmantelle, 1970) has, as background, Levinas's (1969) work on difference/deference and his critique of being. Two profound, prophetic voices, so much to explore.

Hospitality has its frightening aspects. At the beginning of the *Seder*, we offer to open our doors to those in need. And while it is true that each year there are those at the table that might not otherwise have a *Seder*, we would be terrified to let anyone who appeared in. Think of Bunuel's movie *Viridiana*. With luscious Handel's *Messiah* in the background, our heroine of saintly nature tends to beggars and vagrants who reward her by breaking into her cousin's beautiful, wealthy home and, with mesmerising choreography, slowly dismantle it at a banquet that takes the form of the Last Supper. Violence ensues, including violating our caring heroine, who is brought low. Murder, violation, and charity fuse in the unfolding *savoir* that winds through us, as if they are part of a constant conjunction. The raw, captivating images of the movie are packed with possible meaning. You can take it in many directions at once.

Yet, when hospitality works, it is a *mitzvah* that uplifts life, restoring comfort, care, and faith. If only the hospitable moment were a constant. Perhaps, in part, we try to create or reach that moment in therapy, where we hope that all the many forces come together for good, or better than worse, or a worse that is profitable. Maybe we should call them Elijah moments: when we open our *Seder* door and Elijah, who helps our needy selves and raises our spirit, comes in. Although he, too, might be too frightening in his wish to destroy everything wrong with us.

A bit of hospitality playfulness:

To welcome in spite of difference.
To welcome because of difference.
To welcome the stranger who is a neighbour.
To welcome the neighbour who is a stranger.
To welcome the self. (Rumi's host to all inner guests. Rimbaud's I am an other. Whitman's I am multitudes.)

What or who is it possible to welcome and how?
Our psychic immune system has natural resistance. Is it possible to become ill by a toxic welcome one cannot handle? Killed by one's

attempt to welcome what cannot be welcomed? I think of an Isaac Bashevis Singer story of an aged exorcist engaging a mansion haunted by Lilith, the old man found spreadeagled in the snow the next morning. Think of folk tales in which one bites off more than one can chew, one's own digestion becoming indigestible.

Dosage is important, little by little, building capacity to take more over time. How much, with what quality?

What is possible for you now? Twenty years from now? Are you the uncreated one you are waiting for?

God keeps asking, "Where are you?" If He cannot find you, can you?

* * *

Therapy spans many levels, from the catastrophic to ordinary everyday living. In work with psychosis, work with catastrophic elements becomes more explicit. Psychosis is a catastrophe made up of catastrophes, layers upon layers of something gone wrong (Eigen, 1986, 2009). At the same time, psychosis might be a form of communication. Often, the psychosis is treated as something out there, not part of me, something extrinsic that happened to befall me. Yet, it might be a form I took to communicate catastrophic reality. By "form I took", I do not mean something conscious and willed, but more a spontaneous organisation that came about unconsciously, beyond my control. A catastrophic organisation communicating something catastrophic about my existence, my life as catastrophe or catastrophic events that befell with devastating impact. A catastrophic form as a happening and form of communication, a kind of SOS.

For some individuals, this SOS can be going on for years before breaking out and stopping a life ("breakdown"). It can be hidden in banter and busyness. I have met many who led populated lives, needing contact to ward off the dread of terrifying isolation. Contact with others brought some relief, yet inwardly they felt isolated, far away, as if marking time until disaster hit.

Chronically isolated and withdrawn individuals are on the other end of the scale, where being alone is less anxiety raising than being with people. They might be more obviously in difficulty, but use isolation as a defence against disaster, which, nevertheless, past a certain point, may break out and demand help. What is wrong with us builds up and makes itself known, in one form or another. To catch it before it destroys too much life tissue is a stroke of good luck. Yet, there are some who can only find help when almost all life is gone.

Whether addicted to others or oneself, SOS ticks off whether in a black box of an isolation chamber or a bell jar of words. In therapy, the bell jar reverberates, its message trying to get through at last. I think of all the references in the Bible to the dead coming alive, physically or emotionally. The Bible is alive with dramas of affect, the latter's fall and rise, convolutions, involutions. Therapy picks up this thread in human history and brings emotional catastrophe into sustained, person-to-person focus.

I use psychosis as an example, but "impulse" disorders are perhaps even more obvious and devastating. Impulse allied with calculation can play a role in international disasters, for example, premature war. Here, the whole world becomes populated by destructive fantasy made actual, whereas the clinically psychotic are probably behind closed doors (www.psychoanalysis–and–therapy. com/human_nature/eigen/pref.html).

Catastrophic work can go on silently, part of goodness. Mothers idealise babies. It might be a natural tendency to idealise one's children. A mother might be hit hard by reality when loss of sleep, fatigue, and frustration with a thousand things accumulate. Reactions to childcare may be mixed, indeed, and the baby is the recipient of the shifts in moods. But even when mother is feeling good and feels good about the baby, she might or might not know who the baby is. Good feeling may sweep away not knowing. But good feeling is not enough for someone to feel known, in so far as one can be known. A child might feel good feeling spreading through and still feel alone, isolated, unknown. In certain instances, idealisation militates against actually experiencing the child, as Kant might say, as she is in herself. I remember a Tamayo painting called *Happy Mother*, in which a mother holds a baby crucified upon her breasts. To be sure, this mother's expression was more a grimace than happiness, but the point is joined. Happiness and good feeling do not necessarily a baby know. For some, this sense of not being known can be catastrophic, a chronic smouldering catastrophic element in life beneath the good. For others, it might be something one learns to take for granted, part of the way life is.

That does not mean nourishment is not transmitted, just that who is being given to and what is given cannot be taken for granted. Nourishment and catastrophic elements often intertwine (Eigen,

1999). This puts therapists in a quandary. Having good feelings or bad feelings with a patient cannot always be taken at face value. I have seen new therapists surprised at a patient abruptly bolting when the therapist was feeling good about their work and, the corollary, someone a therapist felt bad with might turn out to be a dedicated patient, determined to make use of the situation. What a feeling is or what it might mean keeps unfolding. Situations keep changing. If you jump in too quickly, you might miss what the next moment would bring. On the other hand, if you do not jump in, you might lose the moment. The situation at hand dictates or pressures a response.

Here is a communication Jeff Eaton, author and psychoanalyst in Seattle, sent to my Yahoo! workshop:

> Monday night, the last kid I see before I go home, came into my office a few minutes late. I had some books and papers on the edge of my desk and he flung them on to the floor as he passed by. He then went to the toys and started sorting them (he's eleven).
>
> I felt a flush of anger, but, surprising myself, said nothing. I sat down in my chair and noticed how clearly I felt I did not understand what just happened. What is there to say if you don't know what is going on? He was very purposeful, sorting wild animals, domestic animals, and dinosaurs from a bin of toys.
>
> I felt my anger coexist with some confusion as well as curiosity. I observed him closely. I could "tell" I thought that he was angry from the look on his face, the tension in his actions, the way he didn't look at me. But why? Angry with me? Angry from something before the session? I don't know.
>
> I felt something relax in me as I realised I didn't have to speak or know what was going on. I could just sit and watch and see what happens next. I started to feel a softening in me. And, I started to see a gradual softening in him, too, I could just feel it in the atmosphere.
>
> This all took about fifteen minutes, in silence. Then he looked up at me and said, "You are probably wondering what I am up to."
>
> "Yes," I said, "I'd really like to know."
>
> "It's going to take every ounce of your keen mind to figure it out," he said.
>
> I felt glad he felt I had a keen mind and said, "Well, I'm up for the challenge."

What unfolded was a rather intricate scenario about the farm animals having to prepare for a double assault from dinosaurs and wild animals. The farm animals were divided between the cows who just wanted to stay in the barn and be left alone, the pigs who are arrogant and confused, and the horses who, with the goats, were trying to plan for the attacks. The birds, chicken, and geese were trying to escape, while some wanted to stay and fight. The dinosaurs were bent on pure destruction while the wild animals had other motives, like just getting something to eat.

I made no interpretations but felt moved by all the different motivations at play and made many comments and questions related to each different animal's situation. The session ended with me learning nothing concrete about the interpersonal or real world source of his angry beginning but a much more detailed sense of how complex his inner world might be and all the forces impinging upon him. My goal was not to give him anything, but to learn what I could about his experience.

Jeff's example goes some distance to show that sitting with not knowing, tolerating possible differences between one's reactive "take" and reality, might enable complexities of interest to develop, partly because things are more or other than our "takes". How does one leave room for sitting with reality if a building is burning and one needs to act? Different questions, different moments. Had Jeff reacted reactively, instead of with the disciplined, interested mindfulness he managed, there might have been a burning building instead of an intriguing therapy session.

*   *   *

In much of my practical work, I have associated demonised aspects of the self with self-hate (Eigen, 1993). Brutal self-attack, ripping apart the fabric of self and being become part of "permanent" densities, layers of fathomless self-hate. The devil, often portrayed as envying God's creative power, hating God, becomes a god of the psyche. What often is overlooked is satanic self-hate. The devil expresses a psychical force that Freud partly described as destruction turned against the self. One of Freud's helpful formulae envisions capacity for tendencies to be directed towards outer or inner objects, for example, destruction turned out or in. There can be moments when a destructive tendency seems almost pure, inscribed in language, for example, as "pure hate".

Usually, Freud insists, every psychic act is a mixture of tendencies, for example, mixes of love and hate with shifting balances. Since each tendency can be inner/outer directed, mixes become bewitchingly complex.

In therapy, a gradual shift of balance towards good inner feeling is, I suspect, most often transmitted atmospherically, with words as one expressive vehicle, infused with deeper emotive tones. Words are important and even revelatory. In Jewish folklore, good or bad words can create angels or demons, expressing the spirit in which they are offered. Similarly, therapy words are informed by affective attitudes that have impact over time. The psychical tone and work of good therapy offsets some of the infected self-hate, a chronic inflammation of unconscious life.

In *The Psychotic Core* (1986), I chart movement in dreams from butchered parts of animals in the desert, through terror of invasion (someone breaking in to rape or kill) to gradual easing of destruction. In *Emotional Storm* (2005), there are chapters on dream images, including killers in dreams. Destructiveness does not vanish and perhaps should not—we need its energy in many ways. Bion writes of love and hate as providing different views of reality. There is creative destruction as well as destruction that seems to have no good use that we can see. Suicides of young people—why?! It takes some turn in life and therapy to convert despair and self-hate that rips soul and body apart to a sense of strength and might that infuse attempts at living.

Kabbalah commentary sometimes locates evil in a hypertrophy of *gevurah*, a mixture of judgement, severity, and fear. Jesus taps this: Judge not that ye be not judged (Freud: turning out–turning in, reversal, turning into the opposite, turning against the self). Psychoanalysis often emphasises ameliorating a too severe superego, a self-attacking "conscience", an "immoral conscience" (Eigen 1986, 1996). Bion describes the superego gone mad as an "egodestructive superego", a force that attacks and damages capacities that maintain contact with reality. Sometimes, I wonder if there should be a term underego to complement superego, a force below as well as above that draws the psyche down into it. Then I realise, Freud eventually did suggest such a force as part of the id, a death drive that sucks the psyche towards nothing, undoes unities, prepares the way for the psyche to collapse in on itself, a little like entropy or a black hole.

As mentioned before, Kabbalah writes of earlier worlds falling apart because of imbalance of forces, for example, bad balance between judgement–mercy, judgement without mercy, and mercy without judgment. The idea of balance can sometimes be misleading, if we mean by that something static. We are, perhaps, after more free flow between capacities, better functioning of capacities. When capacities work well, they interact with each other creatively, giving birth to new formations.

Meltzer (1973) spoke of therapy babies, the birth and development of new internal objects that add life, resilience, and value. Ehrenzweig (1993) depicts undifferentiated or pre-differentiated preconscious work in which categories are reshuffled and new ones created. The term fertility runs through many dimensions, part of a penumbra of mating capacities. Some births are easy; they seem to happen of themselves, before you know it. Others are painful, agonising. One way or another, before, during, or after, there is no avoiding aches—aches if you do, aches if you don't. Aching is part of being human. "When two personalities meet, an emotional storm is created" (Bion, 1979; Eigen, 2005) The emotional storm might be the baby, a new thought, or feeling, or sense, a new future. Capacities can love and hate each other, as do partners. I sense something in their background interplay getting ready for something that did not yet happen.

There are moments in which nothing seems good, and moments when part of the heart's heart feels that every work exists to increase mercy. No telling ahead of time what the two together might give birth to.

I think all through life one is in dialogue with something dark in one. The point is for a dialogue to begin, find sustenance, and develop. All capacities contribute, but they are in varying phases of birth and development. Some have been weakened by hardship and trauma or lack of opportunity. Some have undergone deformation. Not all capacities are nourished by a given point in time. Spengler (1991) writes of different cultural souls growing under specific conditions. We are subject to accidents of nourishment and feel lucky when something takes root and breathes life into us, something we can give others.

* * *

Bion writes of a psychotic part of the personality. He also feels a non-psychotic part is always present, although it may take many forms.

Freud described the latter as an observer or witness in the middle of a psychotic storm.

A patient, call him Earl, who had been hospitalised several times and helped somewhat by medication, decided he wanted to get off the medication. I say somewhat, because medication did not keep him out of hospital. At the same time, it helped him live his life between hospital stays until the next episode.

He began with me after his last hospitalisation. We had been working for three years when he began to feel strongly he did not want to be on medication. I work with psychiatrists with medication, as I am a non-prescribing psychologist. I suggested he also talk with his psychiatrist about his wish and see if they could arrange gradual cutting down of the prescription. I do not have a strong opinion as to what is good for a person. I work with people who stay on medication all their lives, others who use medication intermittently, and others not at all. One size does not fit all. Therapy is experimental, exploratory. You never know ahead of time what will work or how. There is no one way of helping.

When I heard him tell me and tell me again that he wanted to get off medication, I felt some trepidation and hovered between support and worry. Was he ready? Could he do it? Could we do it together? What added to the worry was that it was about time for another hospitalisation, roughly every three years, and we were approaching that. He was much better and continued to grow in strength, endurance, and use of himself. He had begun to follow interests, was able to go back to work, and had a couple of enriching affairs. Perhaps most significantly, he was more able to bear periods of loneliness, go through them, and meet them creatively. I do not know if it is true for everybody, but how one meets profound aloneness is crucial for many individuals, all the more so when oscillating between psychosis and creativity.

In the middle of wavering and doubts, there can also be a deep faith at the heart of therapy, an experimental and critical faith, a kind of inner barometer that gives you hints about how the winds are blowing (Eigen, 2012a). I felt an inner surge that was saying, "Yes. Go for it." Not without watchfulness or care, but the inner message was pushing for yes.

Earl ignored my suggestion to make an appointment with his psychiatrist and began taking himself off the meds. Within a month it was done. I personally did not notice much of a change, but he said he felt himself more fully. He was not without pain, but the whirring feeling he feared had not reappeared. "I feel like birds are fluttering in my consciousness but bees and bugs have lessened. Sometimes a wind stirs up the dirt in my mind, blows it all over the place, but I'm OK.

"I walk, a little dizzy, but don't stumble. It's like getting dirt in your eye but it's in your thinking, the way thinking feels. If I wait it out, stay with it, it begins to clear and the expanse is beautiful."

Earl is developing what I call a rhythm of faith, capacity to go through, come through experiences, more tolerance for the build up of states. Melanie Klein writes about psychotic anxieties in early childhood, but does not call an infant psychotic. One reason, I think, is that an infant is able to pass through many states without getting stuck forever in one. The infant can go through heaven and hell and all sorts of combinations without personality organising overly rigidly in one or another direction at first. It takes most individuals time for hell to become dominant and persistent. Earl is recovering or discovering some of the early plasticity that enables going through, rather than getting stuck in, a hardened negative position.

As this was happening he told me an important dream. He dreamt his father was drunk on the bottom floor of the house, so drunk he did not know what he was doing. His father collapsed into a mattress on the floor, which is where Earl slept. Earl witnessed this, at once stymied, mesmerised, and somehow enlightened, as if something that was stuck within him, a congealed dense psychic tumour was being revealed, ready for possible work. He immediately recognised it as a psychotic part of himself, a part he could see, stand outside of, and feel a little freer. The image opened many possibilities: for example, no place to rest, no room for him, the story of a traumatised–traumatising parent, a hurtful one in need, stories of intergenerational trauma waiting to be told. But meanwhile, immediately, an image of stuporous intrusion that arrested but did not consume him. It is now eight years later, and he has never returned to hospital or medication. What we were experiencing was the onset of an area of freedom being born.

Another individual dreamt of a patient of hers in institutional work, a violent drug addict who went in and out of hospital. In the dream, she was calmly talking him down from a violent outburst and he was responding, but the situation was fragile. She felt she was trying to communicate with a psychotic part of herself that held a lot of damaged sensitivity bandaged with reactive anger and withdrawal. It was a relief to talk with this part of herself in a spirit of concern rather than shut out or otherwise push away what this man represented. She felt a little closer to herself, a little warmer, with hope of making more room for her existence. She was worried that she, like this man in real life, would falter, relapse, or not be able to get started, gains subject to loss. He alternated between relatively calmer and more violent periods or, as he put it, having and losing his mind. She was not a violent person, no danger of that, but feared emotional violence to herself. One can be emotionally violent to oneself and one's life without lifting a finger.

*   *   *

Deborah Lowery, a profound seeker and Vermont therapist writes (in my Yahoo! group): "If you are silent enough, the energy of the affect gets through".

This is a special kind of silence, a silence needed for the processing of affect. I once saw a bell in a museum in Ireland. The caption read that this bell was said to have the purest sound in the world. I thought, a sound to reset oneself by, perhaps as the sound of the *shofar* (ram's horn) is meant to do on Yom Kippur. A tuning fork for the soul. But it was a sound I never heard. The bell was on display in a glass case, preserved for viewing but not for hearing. Yet, can we say we never hear it? Can we say that it is not ringing now?

One can, too, imagine it so pure that it is soundless:

> Heard melodies are sweet, but those unheard
> are sweeter; therefore ye soft pipes, play on;
> Not to the sensual ear, but, more endear'd,
> Pipe to the spirit ditties of no tone.
> (Keats, "Ode to a Grecian Urn", ll. 11–14)

Perhaps there are contexts, Deborah Lowery points out, that the word "ditties" takes away from the resonance of the soundless. A deeper soundless than "ditties". I wonder if "whispers" might work, but I doubt it. The poet is viewing a Grecian urn, and writing about the scene that is dramatised on it, that touches his fancy. The pipes that are depicted cannot be heard. They could not be heard when the urn was made and cannot be heard now. They are silent, and yet we feel the music one cannot hear, the deep music of no tone that makes up our beings.

*   *   *

Deborah Lowery writes that she feels an "unheard symphony" rather than "ditties" is closer. She feels that "silence or wordlessness can bring one closer to 'The Real' (O) than words". She recalls the poet Rumi, whose words bring us beyond words. She speaks of a "deep vibration of affect, the tone of silent communion, the felt Real beyond words". She reminds us that even words contemplated in silence can bring us to "the 'feeling tone' of the bell that vibrates into infinity".

Here are some passages she quotes from the chapter "Wordlessness", in *Contact With the Depths*.

> Words, whatever else they are, are gateways to the wordless . . .

> The value of wordless experience has been affirmed since the beginning of recorded words. Is wordless experience possible with the advent of verbal language? Whether or not it is, it continues to be valued, cared for, mined, touched. One of the great functions of poetry is to find (and create) the thrill of the wordless through words. . . .

> Letting something sink in and be part of one is something else, something more. Words are an avenue, a conduit, but at a certain point, wordless processing takes over. One is affected through and through but there is a point where the affected self disappears from view. Wordless, imageless being is all that's left. Processing and digestion goes on outside of awareness. The duality being and non-being loses valence, as does the distinction between duality/nonduality. (Eigen, 2011a, pp. 71, 58, 61)

Deborah Lowery adds, "A thought occurred to me about listening to the soundless music and trying and needing to express it to another person—I thought of the intimate moments, lingering moments, after having sex and lying next to your partner in silent communion, thoughts and feelings to the self yet feeling the other there. It is very similar to certain moments in therapy as well. There are moments when words could almost transgress the moment of communion. A song without words in which feeling is the melody".

*   *   *

Here is a quote from *Faith and Transformation* (Eigen, 2011b) on getting along togther:

> In order to get along together, we have to make room for not getting along together. If you're in a relationship, if you have a partner, you don't get along together all the time. If you get along together 5 percent of the time, it's a good relationship. We have to make room for not getting along. Or not being there. Or being irritable, or whatever it is. But in order for us human beings to get along together, we have to learn how not to get along in a better way. (pp. 5–6)

It is not easy being human. Schopenhauer spoke of being a porcupine, and by that he meant the need to keep an appropriate distance from others. But a problem with being a human porcupine is that most of the quills are inside, not outside, sticking into the self. But even that sounds too outside. Maybe closer is picturing the self as a self-sticking porcupine, piercing itself from deep inside. Hurting deep inside is part of who we are.

A hurt we share, aware of it or not. We are experiential amphibians, so speak, distinct from each other, yet, in intangible ways, also parts of each other, outside and inside each other.

At times, we do not know what to do with the pain. A supervisee of mine once told me about a wonderful experience he had with his teddy bear while high on LSD. He was still coming down from heaven when he saw his most hostile patient for a session. Feeling boundless compassion for the tight man, he felt inspired to give the patient his teddy bear, hoping some of the love would seep through. To his shocked horror, the man promptly ripped the teddy to shreds. "How could he do that!" he exclaimed to me, seemingly not taking in the immense gap between his state and his patient's. He was angry with his patient for not being healed by a moment of beauty and failed to grasp that instead of transfer of love, there was transfer of rage.

This is an extreme instance, but it is not too unusual for therapists to wish patients better and feel complex sets of feelings at slow and difficult work.

Someone else told me of a child needing to tear the insides out of her doll. In this case, the therapist wondered if the little girl was trying to show she had no insides. Another possibility, I thought, was that she might be trying to show how damaged and problematic insides are, an attempt to get the painful insides out of you, attacking the attacker. I suspect often we invisibly attack our painful insides, trying to get rid of them.

I think, too, of the holes drilled in ancient skulls and wonder if they did not have something to do with trying to get bad things out. Perhaps bad feeling, a persecuting force, demon, inner attacker, the thing creating hell in one's head. Or, in the case of turning the whole doll inside out, taking all the insides out, the hell throughout one.

A thread of the Job story might have to do with cutting away everything to get to what cannot be cut away, what must remain. If Job were a modern day patient for whom nothing is real or real enough, we could envision all that he lost—family, business, a good way of life—as feeling unreal (for Job as a partial model for psychotherapy, see Eigen, 1995). A patient might say, "I act as if I'm there, I show affection, I seem to care, but inside it doesn't mean anything to me, I'm frozen, detached." In such a case, neither self nor others are really real and the sense of unreality is painful. Job tries to cut it out, get rid of it. That is one meaning of losing everything, everything dying. One is dying inside.

Another interpretation might see Job's journey as relinquishing attachments. Or another, a mystic's journey, giving up everything in search of God. What is amazing is that Job gets there. He finds the Greatest Intimacy of All. A story about following inner promptings that lead to the Boundless, a drive to do away with everything but contact with God. For him, the intimacy of contacting God on a dung heap, not Mount Sinai (another God meeting, another set of qualities). From the depths of nothingness, seeing, knowing God in his flesh: I know you in my flesh. An ascetic's fable, giving up everything to concentrate and intensify God-contact. Infinite intimacy, Infinite Presence.

It is a journey most of us do not want to take, but perhaps our moods mirror it in some form. Rhythms of contraction–expansion. After Job contacting God in a most distilled, heightened way, crops and animals and loved ones return, a new family, new life, a new attitude. For Job, everything lost, everything gained, a portrayal of an inner drama that goes on incessantly. Stripping away everything to find the point of God-contact, then an expansive movement in which God is everywhere and everything is real. Tearing one's insides out, drilling holes in oneself are transitional phases in a larger movement, phases in which many get stuck. So often, our responses to inner torment increase it, lacking a larger frame of reference.

*   *   *

Another quote from *Faith and Transformation*:

> Faith plays an important role in transformational processes in psychotherapy. I don't mean "belief". Belief may be a necessary part of the human condition but it tends to prematurely organize processes that remain unknown. For me, faith supports experimental exploration, imaginative conjecture, experiential probes. The more we explore therapy, the more we appreciate how much our response capacity can grow. We are responsive beings, for good and ill. Too often, our responses hem us in. We short-circuit growth of responsiveness. Yet it is possible to become aware of the rich world our responsive nature opens, places it takes us, feelings with as yet no name, hints of contact that may never be exhausted. (p. vii)

I have often thought of sessions as crises of faith (Eigen, 1999). Shakespeare often wrote of "good faith", and Lacan, too, uses that phrase. It is a sense expressed in many places, contrasting good or bad faith. Since we are aware of reversals of affect, pronoun, object, and drive, we easily get into hot water by asserting definitive "knowledge" about what is good or bad about the makeup of things: better to tread softly. Bion calls faith the psychoanalytic attitude and associates it with a discipline of abnegating expectation, understanding or desire, an elaboration of Freud's attitude of free-floating attention and abstaining from judging in sessions.

In many sessions, one means something like faith in living— having enough faith to continue life, in contrast with despair, loss of faith, and intensification of the wish to die. Faith as a life or death matter, as well as faith playing a role in the quality of inner life, mood, the taste and tone of existence. One might speak of a heart of faith in contrast with a malignant spirit that poisons life, does one in. A conflict between the two in a single person may be great. In some, struggle against malignancy heightens the heart of faith, and in others, the latter begins to die. Sometimes, when I think of people who killed themselves, I feel they may have tried to preserve some remaining point of faith before it ended, better to die with that precious remnant intact than lose it entirely.

As someone who is a psychologist with an appreciation of mystical experience, the faith I write of is a critical faith, not dogmatic belief. As I wrote in *Faith and Transformation*, faith is deeper than belief. Moses meets God, then expresses it in laws. One can imagine someone else meeting God and expressing it as art, music, poetry, dance, profound silence, shouting, or, as David did in the last psalm, banging the drum and cymbal, overflowing. Or staying, as best one can, with the emotional reality of a psychoanalytic session.

I feel a deep faith in the heart of religions I know, but people fight over belief systems. The deep heart of faith brings us together, the belief of religious systems is territorial, aggressive. Belief functions as a defence against faith as well as a codified (often rigidified) expressive outgrowth of it. Faith as a psychoanalytic attitude is not belief so much as a more open approach towards emotional experience. Can you imagine or sense a critical, appreciative, and open attitude in the face of the birth and development of emotional experience in the immediate appeal of a therapy session?

There are extremes and continua of possibilities. One pole is use of terms like abolishment, abnegation, nullification, shared in varying ways by Freud, Bion, Lacan, and mystical writings. Lacan compares the analyst with a rubbish dump. I have often heard analysts bemoan the fact that a patient does not say anything, dumps, goes on and on, nothing happening. Lacan speaks of a real psychoanalyst overcoming this attitude, more: "it's one he purely and simply abolishes within himself in the exercise of his practice" (Lacan, 1993, p. 39).

Here, Lacan suggests a real psychoanalyst abolishes accusations of the patient, irritation with analysis that is not an analysis, a patient that is not the kind of patient one would like to have, abolishes his feeling that this is rubbish. A real psychoanalyst means one engaged with the realness of analysis, the realness of psyche, of life. What is abolished? An attitude that would make the life of analysis less real? Lacan tells the analyst to abolish his negative attitude towards analysis and the patient's failure to use it.

In the very next paragraph, Lacan's negativity comes out towards his colleagues—he speaks of the rubbish heap of most analytic writings. In psychoanalysis, we suspect nothing gets abolished. Not abolishment, displacement. Or is he saying, abolish negativity with your patient, save your scorn for colleagues.

How to work with one's negativity is an issue of much discussion. The patient pushes buttons. Something inside begins to blow, withdraw, simmer, die, hurt. In "Working with 'unwanted' patients" (1977), I describe what it feels like working with intractability.

Another way of seeing abolishment is free-floating attention, in which Freud says do not judge what is being said, hover evenly, something that might seem like nothing or unimportant might turn out to be a building stone of something crucial.

Abolish judging. This links with the psychoanalytic attitude described by Bion as open faith without memory, expectation, desire, or understanding. Abolish oneself? What is this abolishing?

The *Tanya*, a mystical Jewish text, claims that aspects of the evil inclination cannot be sublimated or transformed or struggled with. They must be abolished. The singular place Freud wrote of losing energy in the closed energy system he postulated was the work of the death drive. Somehow, some energy in the system becomes lost, perhaps a kind of entropy. Something is lost. Is there something about the death drive that is creative, part of creativity, an abolishing that is opening?

To null, abolish oneself, to lose oneself in openness to the moment. To lose oneself in utter nakedness. From antiquity, there is a losing that is finding and a finding that is losing. Jewish mysticism asserts that you and the universe are destroyed and created each moment, infinitesimal infinities of moments.

Lacan: abolish one's disgust with analysis; Bion: one's resistance to the reality of the moment, resistance to psychic reality. An abolishing that is a practice, part of a path.

I have experienced moments like this. Then plain me resurfaces, Mike comes back, warts and all. But in those special moments Lacan calls abolishment, something happens. A further frame of reference begins to take hold. An Archimedean shift. I am not gone forever. Here I am. But there is a difference deep down. A nullification that opens something precious. Something more than anticipated, making me not less, but other, fuller, more ready, more intimate.

*   *   *

We love surfaces and depths. Both have their mysteries and revelations. On Yom Kippur, Day of At-Onement, depths are inexhaustible. Surfaces penetrate them. Everything we have done on the surface of the earth that hurt life echoes in bottomless depths. We are told we can atone, either by asking forgiveness of one we hurt or through God directly.

Humans invent days that condense feeling. At Yom Kippur, feeling bad about oneself, the awful things one did or that happened, the pain that besets one, the fear, the pleas. The idea that, to some extent, penitence is possible, a reversal or turn or change. Condensations of intense feelings of destruction and restoration. Biblical imagery is filled with new life, as if it keeps distilling the ache and tries to wash it out. Cleansing images, new birth images. Fresh start images. Over and over, throughout the stories and prophecies.

There are many ways to relate to life's pain. One is going into it and into it some more. We are spiritual centipedes. We go in and more deeply in. And we also have a capacity to transcend, be outside it, other than it, other than ourselves. There is a beauty in immersion and a beauty in transcendence and all the fusions.

Freud said psychoanalysis has a lot in common with the ancient mystery cults, which emphasised rebirth, renewal. The great theme of dying–living throughout a lifetime, throughout a day. From living to dying, dying to living, in many keys and qualities. Whole worlds of affective experience that "cycle through renewal and destruction many times even in a single day" (quoted from Emma Lunbeck, personal communication). Many times a day, a week, a month, a year seems slow motion when envisioning infinities as a moment.

Bion refers to infra as well as ultra. One can imagine worlds of experience that are not, cannot be experienced, that play out beyond the margins of awareness, infra and ultra events that have an impact outside of that we take to be conscious perception. Experience that is not experienced? What can that mean?

Carol Zeitz, a NewYork psychotherapist, family and marriage counsellor in my private Bion group, spoke of how we are preparing for what has not come, "gathering data for experience that hasn't emerged yet".

In the state I was in, I felt this as something good, the Good Yet to Come, that might be on the way. But she reminded us that it might not be good, which reminded me of Bion's remark about life filled with surprises, most bad. But for me, that moment, it was building capacity for the Good That is Coming. We need capacity not just to endure the bad, but tolerate the build-up of good as well.

Going along with Carol's feeling is the way we are walking danger alarms. Freud wrote of attention searching the outer world for what might sometime be needed for survival and to deal with inner emotional pressures. He also wrote of consciousness as a sense organ for the perception of psychical qualities. We share with animals being wired for danger, food, and sex. Curiosity and exploration often are related to mapping the environment as part of readiness for survival. Freud adds inner emotional pressures, which can include these, but opens further terrain. We have a range of attentional states linked with inner and outer realities, perturbations, qualities, including active, insistent focus, attention drilling inward, rapid scanning, free-floating. Marion Milner (2012) describes a wide, open ended, expansive, almost inattention, kind of attention that often surprises, uplifts, and broadens a sense of being. This last reverberates with Taoist descriptions of inaction.

Bion adds descriptions of how paying attention to almost anything leads to seeing more, learning more. The more attention one gives something, the more one sees. This can be demoralising. Not just the more we learn the more we know we do not know, but also the more bad we see, ever more details and possibilities of negative aspects of personality swim into view. As if attention not only discovers what is there, but creates further possibilities. We have a hunger for everything bad in us.

For some, this goes along with creativity greed, hunger with no end. It might also go along with learning and perceiving for its own sake, hunger for the thing itself. Here, physical survival is less the issue than questions having to do with quality of life, integrity, problems and mysteries of psycho-spiritual being, adventures of thought and imagination, curiosity, and exploration of mental worlds. In a sense, the more we exercise attention, the more attention grows, the more we have for use, including the feeling of attention itself, the multi-dimensional continua of attentional states.

*   *   *

Themes of abundance–scarcity, plenty–drought, fecundity–barrenness run through the Bible on many levels, including physical, psychological, spiritual. On a physical level, there are times of plenty and times of scarcity. Joseph interprets a king's dreams in Egypt and warns him to use the seven good years that are coming to prepare for seven bad ones to follow. Here, abundance–scarcity has to do with food.

When we think of abundance, we think of all the many kinds of vegetation and creatures that populate sea and earth, even dirt and rocks of so many colours. Colour and sound add to the richness of life. If one has known colour and sound and loses sight and hearing, one experiences another contrast of richness–poverty. In such an instance, one may have to dig deeper to find other kinds of richness.

Fecundity–barrenness, having children or not, is a strong biblical concern. There is in the Bible a drive towards abundance, more life, more children, crops, and herds. And implicit in this is a drive towards more God. To be deprived of God's presence can be worse than having no food or children, although all these and more can be complexly connected.

To have more God is connected with having more life. And having more life can mean more feeling and spirit. Physical, emotional, spiritual fecundity or loss. The relationship between dimensions can be complex. Job loses everything to find God more intensely. All capacities are cut away until only God is left: a raw meeting with God.

Joseph is cut away from his family, thrown into a foreign land. A situation that, in a deep, psychological sense, is rather common. Many of my patients find themselves in this predicament. Extremes of familial imprisonment, too much clinging, no air to breathe and/or too premature a break, thrown out of the nest as an infant, banished from closeness. Toxic closeness–toxic distance. Combinations of toxic and healthy closeness–distance sometimes seem baffling, until one relinquishes one's picture of how life "should" be and grows with what is.

To be cut away from one's family and thrown into a foreign land. For another person, this might mean the foreign land of oneself. Cut off from the family of self, thrown into a foreign land of self. It might mean anything from feeling something off to radical dislocation and depersonalisation, feeling unreal to oneself. It might, also, be a challenge, a desperate, creative need to cut away the familiar in order to explore the unfamiliar. Where will creative greed not take us?

Joseph, cut away from his family, prospers in the land of Egypt, working for another. He is a seed blown by the wind that richly grows. A masterful dream interpreter, a capacity that got him into trouble with his siblings, but brought him to great heights in Egypt. And, as fate would have it, his family came to him for sustenance during a time of famine. Again, a basic theme: to have *and* to have not. Joseph had when his family needed. Joseph prospered because of psychological richness and richness of spirit and was ready when his family needed help. Two basic states are being contrasted, one psychologically rich, one psychologically impoverished, a theme that threads its way through the Bible and culture.

When one contrasts full–empty, one has to be careful of context. As language teaches, a person can be full of himself, too full, or full in a wrong way. To say someone is full of himself is close to saying he is full of shit. At the same time, there is fullness of inner riches, my cup runneth over. Likewise, being empty of self or having a self that feels empty has to be contextualised. It is too simple to draw a distinction between positive and negative emptiness, but that helps to get a sense of what is at stake. Creative emptiness, creative void, uncarved block, embryonic, unborn, no-thing—terms linking with potential, staying open, possibility. On a mystical level, sometimes linked with All or Universe or Unknown Happening that keeps happening. On the other hand, there is the emptiness of the lost in spirit, one who is empty of life. Terms can turn many ways.

Joseph, like Jonah, is cast out, grows, incubates, and helps others. The semi-invisible ink in biblical narratives weaves pictures of growth or failure to grow. Keep your eye on the affect. What states are being portrayed, with what kind of weave?

In some two hundred years, as portrayed in the narrative, the Hebrews would fall from high to low. Literature, often unconsciously, expresses basic emotional states as well as external conditions. From low to high and high to low. Empty to full to empty. Dramas of emotional states, what it feels like to be alive, core feeling and spirit. We have an emotional sense. A feeling taster, a feeling sensor-feeler, intimately linked with mood, states of being. Freud informally tied creative flow and blocks to mood. Basic states like high–low, full–empty find their way into common speech, in which we locate ourselves on an emotional spectrum.

Low to high with Joseph. Then gradually lower and lower until, at the lowest point, a rise begins again, the journey to Mount Sinai. Moses, who combines low and high, the most humble man that ever lived, with an anger problem. Inside us is a meeting with God that Moses depicts, not quite as full and splendid as we might like, a meeting that leaves us imperfect as ever, but with a difference. A difference of quality of energy and direction, a subtle, often invisible, thread that reminds us of an inexhaustible cup to drink from.

* * *

Bion calls attention to swings from maximum to minimum emotion (or the reverse) and not just swings, but simultaneity. One can be totally turned on and off at the same time. A lot of Bion's logic is both–and rather than either/or, simultaneous existence of what one might think are opposite states.

The move from maximum to minimum emotion might be something like tripping a circuit breaker. Too much emotion leads to no emotion. In Chapter Two of *Attention and Interpretation* (1970; Eigen, 1998), Bion traced a movement from screaming in response to loss of emotional nourishment through steps that lead to loss of feeling and no scream. I scream, no-scream. It would be worth seeing how the personality comes back, begins to feel and live again. Many of Bion's descriptions involve frustration at therapy not seeming to be therapy and disappointments in living. Sometimes, it seems as if a circuit breaker goes from on to off. Resetting or recharging the self is harder to depict. A double movement, on to off, off to on, the latter often more difficult to achieve.

Bion writes of moments when one gets thrown off. Someone makes a remark that hits home and black winter begins. One moment happily going along, then pow!, a movement from an initial shock of Ouch, through ripples of pain, to off. Resilience or interaction or rest might help reset the psyche and get ready for more. Like day and night, lights and sound lessen, go off, and gradually return, another dawn of the psyche. A kind of death–rebirth process that can happen gradually or on the turn of a coin. Smash, Gone, Return, with whatever ripples crescendos, pianissimos. Resetting the self happens all the time.

Maximum–minimum states are often expressed in both secular and religious literature. A big Yom Kippur theme: children of man, sitting in darkness, afflicted and chained. Then comes God, grace, inner freedom, opening. The Impossible happens repeatedly. The plenitude of the death drive, the poverty of life, reversal after reversal, fusion after fusion. There are creative aspects of the death drive and destructive aspects of the life drive (Eigen, 2012a). The former takes one to many zero states (z-states), plus and minus z. The zero that gives birth and the zero that ends.

For Bion, the resistance of therapist or patient is resistance to reality, emotional or psychic reality, O. Elijah comes sometimes in forms we would not choose, in which the messenger is someone we find abrasive personally or even toxic, but benefit from by the exercise of patience and a sense of the real outside our comfort zone. There is something in keeping a long-range view. There are challenging moments when one has a chance of withdrawing projective needs from a patient who acts un-patiently from one's viewpoint. When a patient acts outside the therapist's comfort zones, he or she might be fighting the therapist's projection, the therapist's picture or idea of the patient that the latter refuses. He/she might be fighting for his/her own inner freedom. Both therapist and patient are enjoined to search more deeply for a fuller O, past mutual projections, even beyond each other's immediate personalities.

As mentioned earlier, Bion uses terms like psychotic or non-psychotic parts of personality. I translate this into affective attitudes. Psychotic affective attitudes are common in everyday life, along with other attitudes. There is no such thing as an attitude without an affect tone. Whether or not there is affect without attitude requires more thought and observation. In practical daily life, probably not, but there might be more pure affect moments. Through meditation or simply by attentional awareness (1995), I may try to help patients get in touch with affect as such. There are benefits to experiencing an affect core past its attitudinal organisation. A moment of pure feeling that feels nourishing and growth promoting. One relaxes into feeling itself rather than remaining feeling-phobic. I have often seen people benefit simply by bathing in a feeling moment, just as it is, without trying to figure it out. At some points, it can be important to build a taste for experiencing and nurture the capacity to let feeling grow, asking nothing more than tolerating emotional nuclei linked with what Winnicott calls going on being.

It is not unusual to try to talk ourselves or each other out of experiencing by prematurely trying to make sense of it, often a sense driven by habitual categories that might miss what is fresh or new in the moment. In therapy, we try to build more tolerance for letting be, making room for differences, even slight differences in the perception of oneself or others. As ever, we are involved in dialectical, paradoxical work. On the one hand, sensitively exposing and working with attitudes embedded in affect and affect embedded

in attitudes, moving between analysis and more nearly pure experiencing.

*   *   *

Response capacity grows in therapeutic work, for therapist as well as
patient. When Sherman Schachter, the head of the clinic in which I
saw my first individual therapy patients, asked how I was doing, I
said, "I don't know about my patients, but I'm getting a lot out of our
sessions." He quipped back, "Well, then, things are going well. At
least someone is getting something."

Support like that made a huge difference in my life as a beginning
therapist. For many years, the feeling that therapy is for therapists was
in the background and later, when someone would ask how I liked my
work, I would joke, "It's great. It keeps me off the streets." Now, I have
been around a lot and gone through so much that it is much harder to
tell who is getting more. Maybe my patients and I are running neck
and neck and it has become obvious even to me, that many have
benefited enormously. Some would not have had lives or been alive
without our work. Of course, there is a wide range of outcomes,
although sometimes even a little is a lot and a lot is too little.

One way therapists and the therapy field grows is by having new
response capacity stimulated by patients. I do not mean simply
stretching or moving past comfort zones in one or another way,
growth producing as this can be. I mean something more—new ways
of responding can evolve under pressure of need.

A case in point is the work of the "borderline". I say work *of* the
borderline rather than work *with* because I mean something analogous
to dream-work, or death-work, or primary process, or alpha work.
There is a kind of "borderline work", ways the psyche learns to work
with individuals who could not be worked with on a widespread,
reliable basis before the psychic work needed to work with them came
into being.

I was a young therapist, and among my patients at the clinic was
a super-sensitive young woman who spoke about PAIN (her capitals,
in the many notes she wrote to me) and the flood of feeling she felt.
Our sessions were emotional floods, jumping from state to state. She
affected me in all sorts of ways and I did my best and often managed
to find paths through the upheaval. I valued her emotional sensitivity
enormously. I would not say I envied it exactly, admiration comes

closer. It seemed to me a precious capacity and made me think of Isaac Bashevis Singer's remark that we are all millionaires in emotions. At the same time, it was clear that emotional turbulence rocked the boat of her life, entailing danger of capsizing. As it turned out, without clear rationale, my own appreciation of the value of her feeling coupled with a steadier hand through the tumult helped her appreciate and use her sensitivity in ways she could not before. Her creative sense of life, art, and writing began to blossom.

Within a few years, I met with what came to be known as more usual "borderlines", sensitive, turbulent, and angry. Beseeching, needy sensitivity that could turn on a coin to hostile sensitivity, irritability that rose to the surface of emotional currents; acute hostile sensitivity as part of reactive immediacy to emotional pain, helplessness, frustration, and need to control. What to do, how to be? I did not know what hit me. I felt I was riding a wild bronco psychically that could easily throw and stamp on me any time. As time went on, I gradually felt less hurt and more responsive in ways unknown to me, as if my insides were learning how to open a secret emotional safe without any clear conscious awareness of it.

I began to learn about a new literature growing up about psychotic-like organisations being used defensively, with individuals going in and out of psychotic-like states, usually not needing hospitalisation, part of a way of being, including fusions of hyper-reactivity and anger. As things turned out, I witnessed parts of the field tussle with this new group, workers divided between Kernberg and Kohut.

By the time I heard André Green (1975) read his watershed paper on borderline dynamics, it was clear that a new therapeutic response capacity was growing. The mixtures of closeness–distance my psyche hit upon spontaneously were already being codified. Following Klein, Winniott, Bion, Fairbairn, and Freud, Green summarised and explicated aspects of a growing intuition that neurosis and perversion were defences against psychotic anxieties, which included combinations of abandonment–intrusion dreads.

In my physiological psychology course in graduate school, we learnt of a mother–baby bird response system that was not something I would forget. The baby bird had to peck the mother in a special spot on her neck in order to kick the mothering response into gear. Without this insistent stimulation on the part of the baby bird, the mother bird would not be mothering. Maybe, I wondered, the borderline's anger had a somewhat similar function, to stimulate growth of emotional capacities in the therapist needed for the kind of responsiveness required. This, I think, began to happen. As the borderline's insistence pecked the needed therapeutic capacity to work with them into being, more therapists began to get the hang, the "feel", of being with these patients and managing to help. Therapist response capacity grew.

The so-called "borderline" had the positive role of stimulating further levels of response capacity in aspects of the therapy world. The raw sensitivity of the client stimulated growth of responsive capacity in the therapist. So much so, that in time some began to speak of "borderland" as an avenue of access to aspects of creativity, a steady emphasis in Winnicott and Jung.

In the case of the borderline, the therapy field evolved to develop responses needed by the client. The work continues today, as there are whole categories of people that might require response ability that has not yet arrived. One such involves psychopathy. We live in age in which psychopathy of one or another form is rampant, including in high places of the economic–political ladder (Eigen, 2006). If we fail to learn how to treat this inflammatory social, as well as individual, problem, we might be in big trouble, even more than now.

I feel that we have the resilience, plasticity, and capacity to grow to meet what seems beyond us now. We can work with many kinds of difficulties that once we could not. There is no reason why growth of capacity should not continue. Bion's response to Macbeth asking the physician, "Canst thou not minister to a mind diseased?" was, "Not now perhaps but come back in 200 years and we'll see what we can do." Buddha, when asked by a follower how he was able to reach such a level of achievement, responded, "I've been born millions of times and had millions of teachers." Sometimes, a moment seems like a million years. Yet, lifetimes of moments seem short indeed.

Often I see our whole field as a single therapist. Someone who could only go so far with me might appear in your office and vice versa. Together, we are growing response capacities that many thought might not be possible or envisioned. We are exploring, opening reality together, creating each other.

* * *

The theme of prostration came up in one of our Yahoo! group interchanges. I read the work of a Zen master who advocated beginning the day with 108 prostrations. As soon as I read this, something unyielding in my chest melted. It is not a practice I can follow literally, but even the sense of it began to thaw rigidity. When I do deep bows, I feel a heart sense all through my body, implicit rededication, profound devotion, sometimes quiet longing, caring. A prostrate heart, cushioned by the whole body. As I write this, words come: "You are my Peace."

Such moments help reorientate, reset, the self, one's attitude, one's sense of being. But difficulties do not vanish for long. Before my first trip to Seoul, I received more writings of the Zen master mentioned above. He had been in Providence and New York and now was believed to be outside Seoul in a monastery I was to visit. In one of his writings, he mentioned a heart problem. Doctors advised medication, which he refused. He felt meditation would do the trick. He said curing himself of his heart ailment was not what meditation was most deeply for, even if it could be used that way.

You can imagine my surprise when I arrived at the monastery and found he had perished of his heart problem and a new teacher had taken his place. As it turned out, my son, wife, and myself had a good meeting with the new teacher and, at its end, he proposed a task for my wife and son while I gave my seminars. He suggested they search for and find a certain statue of a Buddha of Compassion (equivalent of Kwan Yin) in the countryside, a task that turned into an enlivening adventure.

If you are looking for prostrations and meditation to save you from illness and death or as good luck charms, you are missing its true use, which is, in part, to take you to places you might not have found otherwise. Even an accomplished Zen master can miss the mark at times.

Here is another set of feelings evoked by prayerful prostration, different but related, by Rachel Berghash, writer and teacher, on the Yom Kippur service:

> The Carlebach shul I go to focuses on singing. There was an explosion of energy to the singing this year, and the Sh'ma sung by everyone had a special resounding transcending power. While atoning I felt more than a tinge of joy, and when prostrating I felt a deep connection to and love for God and others. I love prostrating when praying, and think of Moslems lucky to practice that. Prostrating is comforting,

humbling, visceral as well as spiritual/emotional. To start the day with 108 prostrations is inspiring.

The last psalms end in banging the drums, dancing, blowing the *shofar*: I imagine shouts, cries of joy. There is no contradiction between this wholly embodied form of worship and expressiveness and standing, silent prayer, speaking the words so only you can hear, you and your Love.

Deborah Lowery associates prostrations with giving thanks, something foundational, touching "the essence of the thing itself", and feels "they would be a wonderful practice in the course of the practice of any faith".

Jeffrey Eaton says of his Buddhist practice,

The teacher is showing us that there is something precious, and much more important somehow, than the habits of the ego. When one encounters that natural dignity and wordless energy of compassion, generosity, wisdom, insight, playfulness, the most natural thing is to bow, not as a sign of submission, but because the ego clears the space for the play of some different level of reception, transmission, and realisation. The most foundational ideas are the teacher, the teaching, and the community. When I bow to the three jewels now I am bowing to the reality that awakening is possible, that there are instructions and encouragement to explore this truth, and that I can learn from "all my relations" and all my interactions, moment to moment, day to day.

I forget about what I "know" from experience, but, then it comes back. And now, when I do full prostrations before morning meditation, it somatically anchors that recognition of humility and awe at the mystery of creation. I think that is why these are foundational practices. Not something to get through or beyond, but, because like every one of Buddha's teaching, they are a gate to "the thing in itself", to the Dharmakaya.

I have not completed my foundational practices, having not accumulated all the prescribed prostrations; on the other hand, the experience has been very generative and whatever part of the practice I do I find deep openings to new perceptions.

In another context, Jeffrey Eaton adds, "One's interpretations can obscure the perception of the moment of grace".

Nuala Flynn, an East London depth psychologist writes (Yahoo! group),

> I have been spontaneously compelled to prostrate for about the past nine months, and it needs to be on grass, either in my garden or in the woods—the smell of the earth and the darkness and depth in it and the deep gratitude and mystery—getting as low as is possible. I don't understand it, I just need to; I feel like a baby in the arms of great mother sometimes, she's as happy to hold me as I am to be held—surface to surface, maximising surface skin contact—although I'm not naked! Not yet!

Shomer Zwelling adds, "As for prostrations, when I teach yoga classes, I end with approximately 15–20 minutes of variations on *savasana* (corpse pose), very relaxing and meditative, resting in peace".

What can prostration and deep devotion mean? Here are some words that come:

> I find my peace in You
> You fling me
> Into the depths
> Over Your shoulder
> Behind Your back
> Down down
> Mountain after mountain
> No stop in sight

*   *   *

There is deep devotional feeling in life. Perhaps not everyone feels it. Some may be so wounded that such feeling is mocked. Not only because it is frightening, but also because it has proved to be ghastly, wounding to the extreme, radically disillusioning.

Perhaps I am wrong, perhaps not everyone would feel it even in the best of circumstances. Sometimes, people try to equate this devotional sense with good parenting. But I have known people with awful parenting to have it, sometimes even more. The birth of the Kabbalah is associated with suffering, exile, historical trauma. One might wonder if agony were not a necessary ingredient to the devotional spirit.

Then again, what kind of devotion? My bias is toward a devotion that is life-affirming, that raises the quality of being, expressing the full organ of the human heart. But what of devoted soldiers killing Jews in the Holocaust, devoted to the fatherland or motherland? Devotion to a lethal cause? What kind of devotion is this? Can one be devoted to murder? I have seen, in deep pathology, trauma increase clinging and masochistic devotion. We have learnt by now the conjunction of sadism and masochism and bonds that damage. We have even learnt that what one person calls damage another calls freedom.

A nexus of states swim together, devotion, faith, loyalty, and sincerity among them. It might be that each can work positively or negatively, depending on spirit, end, and circumstance. Blind faith and devotion mixed with habit and conditioning can bind one to untenable situations, situations that harm oneself or others. Sometimes, what we call a path of least resistance, or inertia, plays a role, sometimes, something more insidious or hard to pin down. Given the complexity of the mind or psyche, things can become complex indeed. Can one tell where a moment might lead? "Thou shalt know them by their fruits". Evidence based faith? Can one judge?

In various of my works, I have described a split or division that can enter myriad dramas. In the chapter, "Words" in *Feeling Matters* (Eigen, 2007), I delineate a moment, perhaps even in infancy, when a head-mind or eye-mind (Elkin, 1972, "transcendental ego/body ego; eye-mind/mouth mind") can become so sharp-edged and acute, that it can watch aspects of the body self go under, dissolve, disappear. In "Words", a patient, Harry, maintains a cutting consciousness as his emotional self goes under, in effect watching a part of himself die. Upper mind, eye-mind goes on ticking while emotional self drowns, sometimes in its own flood. This is a dramatic instance of consciousness going on thinking as emotional life fades into unconsciousness, an emotional unconscious. I wonder and am tempted to posit that with persistent mental consciousness, even as a baby, one can watch as one's emotional self goes under.

I started seeing Harry after one of his hospital stays. After months of work, he determined to get off medication as he felt it dulled the edge of his mind. I wondered if he missed watching himself die or feared not being there if he came alive. Harry felt that words killed but no one around him died when he spoke. He felt he had no impact. His words had no impact; his feelings had no impact. Looks can kill and words can wound or, as Freud noted, a look or word can be experienced as a blow to the face, a stab in the heart. We worked for many years as he slowly came together, sorting out the materials of personality. He was never hospitalised again and eventually became free of medication.

Here is a moment when we began to thaw out together. We were sitting quietly, listening to our breathing. There is noise outside. My office is on the ground floor facing the street.

> A child cries and a mother chastens it, a delivery man chains his bicycle to the bars of my window. Harry breaks into tears. How language captures the sense of breaking, breaking open, breaking down, breaking up, breaking free. He finally broke down, I heard someone say of a man weeping at a funeral.
>
> Harry weeps and weeps and says, 'The mother yelling at the child was too much. When I heard the bike chains I thought, she is chaining the child. I have an urge to step outside and breathe, to unchain the child. I want to give that mother a softer voice. When I hear her voice I stop breathing. My soul stops breathing. My breath contracts around the pain. I'm breathing cautiously, breathing around the pain. Around bullet sounds, bullet words. My breath cushions the shots . . . Now my chest is starting to relax. Soul is in my chest, returning through my chest.'
>
> I too cringed at the mother's metallic, scraping tone. To scold, to make cold. I could feel my insides tightening, soul tightening, all through my body. A tongue lashing is a kind of beating. The emotional and physical meld. When Harry and I thawed out some, my hand involuntarily went to my heart.
>
> Harry did not have to draw blood to see soul. He knows words encode and create affect, are parts of emotional fields. Some people do have to draw blood in order to feel soul. Words are a kind of emotional blood. There is soul in words. (pp. 45–46)

There is soul in words and words can kill soul. As Jewish folklore says, words can create devils and angels. Words not only can express feeling, but create feeling. In therapy, we can give mother a softer voice.

A few moments later, Harry and I fear that the child outside has stopped breathing. We breathe around the pain, contract, find ways of surviving, moving on, carrying many crosses of pain throughout our beings. Everything is in a breath. There might be a way we stop breathing, never breathe again. Feeling has breath as well as taste buds. We might go on breathing physically in restricted ways, enough to get by, but emotional breath and taste may be damaged. Can you imagine a person who has stopped breathing emotionally? I have worked with people where this is so, and know places in myself where this is so.

What is happening with Harry in the tiny incident above? It is one moment in which he is coming alive in a new way. A moment in the birth of experience. In this case, trauma-feeling, trauma-vision, but not only. He feels the moment through and through. This in itself is birth, birth of feeling, vision, birth of moments. We are together resonating to sound, shrill yelling, metal chains. Sound runs through our bodies, giving birth to image and emotional vision, psychic sensing. Something is happening. We are together alone, permeable, ready for more.

*   *   *

The theme of the double has been with us since antiquity. Lovers the result of a prior whole being cut in half, good and bad brothers, including fratricide, God and Satan, creators and destroyers, Kabbalah is filled with many kinds of doubleness and movement beyond oppositions, good and evil inclinations: the psychoanalyst, Melanie Klein, depicts a good and bad breast. Bifurcations run through experience or, perhaps, are ways of trying to organise experience. Doppelgangers, avatars, counterparts, twinships, the list grows.

One coupling I would like to highlight at the moment involves nourishment. In some ways, we are nourished, in some ways not. One can sense a more or less happy baby inside and another on the verge of starvation. If I were an artist, I would depict the two babies within, living, nearly dying, intertwined. Imagine, to be nearly dying all life long. Imagine we have a runt of the litter inside and, perhaps, many corpses as well (Eigen, 2007, Chapter Ten).

Writers in Europe used to depict America as a robust, young, healthy baby and Europe as old, decrepit, *fin de siècle* tiredness, loss of vitality. No accident, perhaps, that one of Freud's concerns as the twentieth century approached, was psychaesthenia (Eigen, 1993, Chapter Nine).

A twinship of nourished–malnourished or undernourished. Is it possible, also, to be overnourished? One thinks of athletes using chemicals to build body muscle, but also many other instances, for example, financial gorging and starvation, a kind of economic bulimic–anorexic tendency. Our society has been depicted both by friends and enemies as bloated, filled with ego, depleted of soul. Such characterisations are extreme, stereotypic. Reality is so mixed that aspects of our life can be enlivening and deadening.

But think for a moment. What truly nourishes you? How are you starving? You might give different answers at different times. Thoughts might come that surprise you. I would like to suggest meditating on the thriving and starving babies. There might be many kinds. You might feel them inside your body, through your skin, in varied organs. Or you might depict them as felt currents or images. Sense the family of babies in you, their relationships or lack of relationships, their tone and temper. Feel what they want to tell you, give you, ask you.

It might be, at some moment, that one turns into the other or that both coincide and become indistinguishable. One might sense benefi-cent and catastrophic aspects of life simultaneously.

I have often heard of one sibling in a family doing well and another terribly. In many families, all the children do well or terribly or everything between. But here I am thinking of the case when one prospers and the other goes downhill. Were they both not nourished by the same parents? In some sense, we learn from psychoanalysis, that siblings have somewhat different parents owing to a host of factors, including birth order and timing. But extremes are striking: a schizophrenic child and a healthy child. Or a child who grows up and makes a go of it and the other fails to work or love and in middle age is taken care of by parents until the latter die.

Recently, I heard of one such instance when the healthier brother sought therapy. He felt peeved at all the attention his helpless brother received from their parents. Almost as if being out of the house, work-ing, married was a lack compared with what he imagined his middle-aged brother was getting. Instead of wiping his brow in relief and feeling, I escaped a sinking ship, he seemed glued to what he was missing as the ship went down. His life was so much better than his brother's, what was he envying or feeling he was missing? His anger tied him in knots, resenting what he could not have. Would he really have wanted to switch positions in order to get what he imagined his brother was receiving? Was an undernourished baby in him craving care?

In one of my thought-images, I found myself thinking or saying something like, "To be an adult means loss as well as gain. Maybe you see your brother as not losing anything? He has your parents and that is everything? But it was not enough for you. You left, came to New York, do good work, have a wife who cares—but none of this is the parental love you imagine. None of this fills a hole left empty by parental love you did not have. The love you had was not enough, or not good enough. When you see your brother cared for like a helpless baby, you don't see his sorry plight, but what you are missing. Are you sorry that you became an adult and he remained a baby? Are you afraid a baby in you needing nourishment will be left behind? You feel it has been left behind and you are angry."

Perhaps that is a price we pay for adulthood—loss of childhood and loss of parental love we never had and never will have, imagined or real. Or perhaps there is survivor's guilt: the film, *Ordinary People*, in which one brother survives, one drowns. Do you feel you should have stayed home and drowned too? Perhaps we have dual tendencies, one to move forward, one back. We miss what we do not have, whether past, present, or future. In adulthood, we do have a chance to build up inner parents within, healthier and fuller, more able and giving. We become more aware of the nourished and undernourished twin-self, and do what we can for self-care, acknowledging a "Siamese twin" aspect of experience. We build the inner parental couple a little at a time, piecing a better feeling together from bits of good feelings we get now. Experience now matters and can go some way not only to making up for loss in the past, but finding places one could not have guessed at before. A certain kind of mourning may be necessary, but at least as important is valuing possibility now. And by possibility I don't mean just active choices, but sources of sustenance we did not know existed, resources that sometimes seem to come from nowhere.

* * *

Bion often writes of catastrophic processes. He uses specific images such as the big bang to evoke a sense of explosive breaking up or down or through. The first four chapters of *Damaged Bonds* (Eigen, 2001b) go along with Bion's (1994) writings about aborted or damaged dream-work. Two quotes from *Damaged Bonds*: (1) "Dreams try to represent what hurts and weave a wombing effect around it, but the womb keeps breaking apart" (p. 43); (2) "The dream distills basic affect states and situations" (p. 55)

Does psychosis also do this, distil basic affect states in frozen–explosive and sometimes semi-fossilised ways?

Bion (1970, Chapter Two; Eigen, 1998, Chapter Three) spoke of baby as bomb in certain contexts. He also wrote of a psychic big bang involved in creation of the psychic universe, a catastrophic creation (O). A catastrophe (O) that also leads to psychotic dispersal–rigidity, in which psychic products (thoughts, feelings, sensations) fly away from each other with increasing velocity, so that they no longer can be thought or felt or sensed. A psychic big bang, a bomb of bombs. Note that the explosion of creation, a big bang, is also used as an image for psychic creation or disintegration, birth of the psyche and its dispersal.

Is psychosis limited to "clinical psychosis"? Can hallucination be invisible and unconsciously shared socially?

A quote from Bion that links personal and social madness:

> Any particular religion changes with the prevalent fashion, but the fundamental thing, religion itself, does not. It is a very powerful force, as can be seen by the evidence of what would appear to be a sign or symptom of the thought of a period dug up by the archaeologists who excavated the Death Pit of Ur. Apparently, when the ruling authority died, the court also died with him; they were all buried in the same pit and took the same dose of whatever was used before they were buried alive. That in itself would seem to suggest that the religious force is a very powerful one, whether it is located in God, or the people, or the priesthood, or the court authorities. (1994, p. 374)

A central element that comes across via Melanie Klein (1946) is that persecutory distress is intrinsic to the human condition. The psyche is, in part, a persecutory psyche. One is persecuted by one's own drives, in this case a destructive drive. Our own psyche is a source of distress.

One can paint a bigger picture involving sources of social, environmental, and biological factors that play roles in traumatic impacts. But Klein argues for inclusion of inherent psychic factors as part of the pool.

Her palette includes mixtures of pain and pleasure, bad and good objects, death and life feeling, varied affect-ego states and structures, with the colours of destructive tendencies part of the mix.

You might say environment can play up or mitigate inherent stress of personality on itself. And environmental factors can play a key role in inducing chronic deformations. But, from a Freud–Klein perspective, even perfect parenting would not eliminate disturbances that beset the human soul. (In any case, the idea of perfect anything can be persecutory as well as comforting or inspiring.) My mother called some of the pains I experienced as a child "growing pains". I suspect the very process of growth can be radically painful at times. Imagine what it might feel like to you now if you went through, in some analogous way, all the growth and changes an embryo or foetus does. What would such a state cost to live through?

On the other hand, a mystic might feel that infinities of development are happening every moment. We might not have access to them, but if we exclude what we cannot access, we would exclude most of the universe and ourselves. We might posit dimensions of unconscious sensing close to birth of experience. Freud, in part, describes consciousness as a sense organ for perceiving psychical qualities. We can extend that to unconscious work as well. It is a thrill to sense birth of experiencing, even vague intimations, unconscious rumblings, stillness that drops us into a well without bearings; unconscious stillness that supports our psychical being before cutting us in half and cutting the halves into pieces. Some pieces are screaming, some filled with joy. We are somewhat dazed with possibility, not sure where or how to go. We get the idea, let's just sit and be with the ruckus for a while, enjoy the quiet underpinning, until a current takes us and we feel like moving.

Over and over a hard to pin down sense keeps asking, "What does it feel like to be alive?" I do not know if it is ever satisfied with any answers. There are so many echoes of the question. A hard to pin down sense sinking deeply into the next moment, beyond hostility and hospitality and formalities of welcome. A wonderful word in English: well-come. To be well, to come, to come well: a well echoing through many levels of being. In the Bible, Isaac, bearer of trauma, is known for digging wells. A link between experiencing the edge of death and faith and coming through in whatever form one can, chastened, alert, aware that more is on the way.

Therapy is one of the places you become aware of how loaded words are. Words are loaded with life, and, for the life form we are, filled with imagination that cannot stop digging wells, looking for ways out or in, creating traps, holes to fall into and explore.

A patient recently marvelled that no matter what happens to him in daily life, his dreams go on ticking images and scenes, checking in to see how he is doing, but not quite waiting for him to catch up. The future is like going for a walk with someone you cannot quite keep up with. One learns a lot about pain as yet unseen but cannot entirely suppress the thrill of speeding downhill on one's psychic sled, still a child. Where are you taking me? I do not know. But I am not quite ready to stop.

REFERENCES

Arieti, S. (1974). *Interpretation of Schizophrenia.* New York: Basic Books.

Arieti, S. (1976). *Creativity: The Magic Synthesis.* New York: Basic Books.

Balint, M. (1992). *The Basic Fault: Therapeutic Aspects of Regression.* Evanston, IL: Northwestern University Press.

Berdyaev, N. (1944). *Slavery and Freedom.* New York: Charles Scribner's Sons.

Bettelheim, B. (1961). *Paul and Mary.* New York: Doubleday.

Bion, W. R. (1970). *Attention and Interpretation.* London: Karnac, 1984.

Bion, W. R. (1979). Making the best of a bad job. *Bulletin of the British Psychoanalytic Society,* February. Also in *Clinical Seminars and Four Papers,* 1987.

Bion, W. R. (1984). *Second Thoughts: Selected Papers on Psychoanalysis.* London: Karnac.

Bion, W. R. (1989). *The Grid and Caesura.* London: Karnac.

Bion, W. R. (1991). *A Memoir of the Future.* London: Karnac, 2004.

Bion, W. R. (1994). *Cogitations.* London: Karnac.

Bion, W. R. (1997). *Taming Wild Thoughts.* London: Karnac.

Chuang Tzu (1964). *Chuang Tzu: Basic Writings,* B. Watson (Trans.). New York: Columbia University Press.

De Chardin, T. (1959). *The Phenomenon of Man.* London: Collins.

Derrida, J. (1978). *Writing and Difference*, A Bass (Trans.). Chicago, IL: University of Chicago Press.

Derrida, J., & Dufourmantelle, A. (1970). *Of Hospitality (Cultural Memory in the Present)*, R. Bowlby (Trans.). Stanford, CA: Stanford University Press.

Ehrenzweig, A. (1993). *The Hidden Order of Art: A Study in the Psychology of the Artistic Imagination*. Berkeley, CA: University of California Press.

Eigen, M. (1977). On working with 'unwanted' patients. *International Journal of Psychoanalysis, 58*: 109–121. Reprinted in Eigen, 1993.

Eigen, M. (1981). The area of faith in Winnicott, Lacan and Bion. *International Journal of Psychoanalysis, 62*: 413–433. Reprinted in Eigen, 1993.

Eigen, M. (1986). *The Psychotic Core*. London: Karnac, 2004.

Eigen, M. (1992). *Coming Through the Whirlwind*. Wilmette, Il: Chiron.

Eigen, M. (1993). *The Electrified Tightrope*, A. Phillips (Ed.). London: Karnac, 2004.

Eigen, M. (1995). *Reshaping the Self*. London: Karnac, 2013.

Eigen, M. (1996). *Psychic Deadness*. London: Karnac, 2004.

Eigen, M. (1998). *The Psychoanalytic Mystic*. London: Free Association Books.

Eigen, M. (1999). *Toxic Nourishment*. London: Karnac.

Eigen, M. (2001a). *Ecstasy*. Middletown, CT: Wesleyan University Press.

Eigen, M. (2001b). *Damaged Bonds*. London: Karnac.

Eigen, M. (2002). *Rage*. Middletown, CT: Wesleyan University Press.

Eigen, M. (2004). *The Sensitive Self*. Middletown, CT: Wesleyan University Press.

Eigen, M. (2005). *Emotional Storm*. Middletown, CT: Wesleyan University Press.

Eigen, M. (2006). *Lust*. Middletown, CT: Wesleyan University Press.

Eigen, M. (2007). *Feeling Matters*. London: Karnac.

Eigen, M. (2009). *Flames from the Unconscious: Trauma, Madness, and Faith*. London: Karnac.

Eigen, M. (2011a). *Contact With the Depths*. London: Karnac.

Eigen, M. (2011b). *Eigen in Seoul (vol 2): Faith and Transformation*. London: Karnac.

Eigen, M. (2012a). *Kabbalah and Psychoanalysis*. London: Karnac.

Eigen, M. (2012b). On Winnicott's clinical innovations in the analysis of adults. *International Journal of Psychoanalysis, 93*: 1149–1459.

Eigen, M. (2013). Response by Michael Eigen. *International Journal of Psychoanalysis, 94*: 118–121.

Eigen, M. (2014). *A Felt Sense: More Explorations of Kabbalah and Psychoanalysis*. London: Karnac.

Eigen, M., & Govrin, A. (2008). *Conversations With Michael Eigen*. London: Karnac.

Elkin, H. (1972). On selfhood and the development of ego structures in infancy. *Psychoanalytic Review, 59*: 389–416.

Fairbairn, W. R. D. (1954). *An Object Relations Theory of the Personality*. New York: Basic Books.

Federn P. (1957). *Ego Psychology and the Psychoses*. London: Maresfield Reprints.

Freud, S. (1937c). Analysis terminable and interminable. *S.E., 23*: 211–253. London: Hogarth Press.

Green, A. (1975). The analyst, symbolization and absence in the analytic setting (on change in analytic practice and analytic experience). *International Journal of Psychoanalysis, 56*: 1–22.

Henle, M. (1971). *The Selected Papers of Wolfgang Kohler*. New York: Liveright.

Klein, M. (1946). Notes on some schizoid mechanisms. In: M. Klein, P. Heimann, S. Isaacs, & J. Riviere (Eds.), *Developments in Psycho-Analysis*. London: Hogarth Press, 1952.

Koffka, K. (1963). *Principles of Gestalt Psychology*. New York: Hourcourt Brace and World.

Lacan, J. (1993). *The Seminar of Jacques Lacan Book III: The Psychoses 1955–1956*, J.-A. Miller (Ed.), R. Grigg (Trans.). New York: W. W. Norton.

Leiner, M. J. (2004). *Living Waters—The Mei Hashiloach: A Commentary on the Torah by Rabbi Mordechai Yosef of Itbitza*, B. P. Edwards (Ed. & Trans.). Lanham, MD: Jason Aronson/Rowman & Littlefield.

Levinas, E. (1969). *Totality and Infinity: An Essay on* Exteriority, A Lingus (Trans.). Pittsburgh, PA: Duquesne University Press.

Levinas, E. (1999). *Alterity and Transcendence*. New York: Columbia University Press.

Mahler, M. S., Pine, F., & Bergman, A. (2000). *The Birth of the Human Infant: Symbiosis and Individuation*. New York: Basic Books.

Matt, D. C. (Trans.) (2004). *The Zohar* (Pritzker Edition). Stanford, CA: Stanford University Press.

Meltzer, D. (1973). *Sexual States of Mind*. Strathtay, Perthshire: Clunie Press.

Milner, M. (2012). *Bothered by Alligators*. London: Routledge.

Plath, S. (1963). *The Bell Jar*. New York: Harper, 2006.

Rank, O. (1932). *Art and Artist: Creative Urge and Personality Development*. New York: W. W. Norton.

Read, H. (1965). *Icon and Idea: The Function of Art in the Development of Human Consciousness*. New York: Shocken Books.

Schreber, D. P. (2000). *Memoirs of my Nervous Illness*. New York: New York Review of Books Classics.

Scott, W. C. M. (1975). Remembering sleep and dreams. *International Review of Psycho-Analysis, 2*: 253–254.

Wiener, J. (2011). *The Way of the 4th Toe: Into the Feeling Body*. Bloomington, IN: I-universe.

Winnicott, D. W. (1953). Transitional objects and transitional phenomena. *International Journal of Psychoanalysis, 34*: 89–97.

Winnicott, D. W. (1969). The use of an object and relating through identifications. *International Journal of Psychoanalysis, 50*: 711–716.

Winnicott, D. W. (1988). *Human Nature*. London: Free Association.

Winnicott, D. W. (1992). *Psychoanalytic Explorations*, C. Winnicott, R. Shepherd, & M. Davis (Eds.). Cambridge, MA: Harvard University Press.

Zalman, S. (1973). *Likutei Amarim: Tanya*. Brooklyn, NY: Kehot Publication Society.

INDEX

For Product Safety Concerns and Information please contact our EU
representative GPSR@taylorandfrancis.com
Taylor & Francis Verlag GmbH, Kaufingerstraße 24, 80331 München, Germany

www.ingramcontent.com/pod-product-compliance
Lightning Source LLC
Chambersburg PA
CBHW050520280326
41932CB00014B/2397